Work

on

Women

# Work on Women

## A GUIDE TO THE LITERATURE

MARY EVANS
AND
DAVID MORGAN

TAVISTOCK PUBLICATIONS
LONDON AND NEW YORK

*First published in 1979 by*
*Tavistock Publications Ltd*
*11 New Fetter Lane, London EC4P 4EE*

*Published in the USA by*
*Tavistock Publications*
*an associate company of Methuen, Inc.*
*733 Third Avenue, New York, NY 10017*
*© 1979*
*Typeset by Inforum Ltd, Portsmouth*
*Printed in Great Britain*
*by J.W. Arrowsmith Ltd, Bristol*

ISBN 0 422 77130 9 (hardback edition)
ISBN 0 422 77140 6 (paperback edition)

British Library Cataloguing in Publication Data
Evans, Mary
    Work on women. – (Social science paperbacks).
    1. Women – Bibliography
    I. Title II. Morgan, David, *b. 1937*
    III. Series
    016.30141'2    Z7961    79–40996

ISBN 0–422–77130–9
ISBN 0–422–77140–6 Pbk

# Contents

Preface   vii

Feminism and the women's movement   1

Domestic life and labour   13

Women and paid work   20

Health, education, and welfare   28

Law and politics   35

Crime and deviance   39

Literature, art, and popular culture   45

Cross-cultural studies   50

Social psychological perspectives   58

Additional bibliographies, general reviews of literature,
feminist journals and periodicals   67

Author index   76

# Preface

This bibliography is intended as a guide to the rapid accumulation of writing and research that has accompanied the women's movement and contemporary feminism in the west. Over a relatively short period of time, and after decades of indifference and neglect, the study of women has developed from a minority interest into a major area of activity and debate. The sources compiled in this work indicate the diversity of current interests and research, but at the same time cover only a small proportion of the numerous publications, papers, and reports that have recently appeared in print. To list all these publications would have produced a work of pointless and unmanageable length; instead, we have attempted to draw together contributions to feminist writing which collectively illustrate the issues and direction of current research and debates.

Most of these issues have an interdisciplinary character which cuts across the conventional boundaries of academic subjects. For this reason we have organized the bibliography not in terms of academic divisions but around the institutional structures that directly affect the pattern of women's lives – education, employment, domestic labour, welfare, politics, the law, medical care, the media, and so on. Each of these sections draws upon a wide range of sources to illustrate different aspects of and perspectives on the problems explored. Much of the work originates from the social sciences, whereas contributions from the humanities and life sciences have so far been relatively small. Similarly, most of the literature is concerned with the position of women in industrially advanced societies in the west. Although we have included comparative material on women in socialist and developing countries, this emphasis is apparent in most of the sections, with a particular bias towards Britain and the United States.

While this edition has been compiled mainly as a resource for women's studies programmes in colleges, universities, and schools, we hope it will be of use to all those with an interest in the women's movement and the literature it has produced. Much of this literature is now generally available, however readers without access to university or college libraries may find it difficult to obtain certain journals and reports. For those with more specialized interests we have supplemented the text with references to additional bibliographies on specific areas and themes. Inevitably, in a subject as broad as this, there are bound to be omissions and gaps, but while the bibliography is not exhaustive, we hope it will introduce readers to the scope and direction of recent work and encourage further explorations, polemic, and research.

Finally, we would like to thank Barbara Haber of the Schlesinger Library and members of the Institute of Independent Study at Radcliffe College, Harvard, for their help and advice.

M.E.
D.M.
April, 1979

# Feminism and
# the women's movement

The contemporary women's movement is the most recent expression of a tradition of feminism whose intellectual origins lie in the sixteenth and seventeenth centuries. Historically this tradition owes much to the rise of Protestantism and the secular extension in post-Reformation Europe of the idea of spiritual equality and freedom central to the doctrines of the Protestant church. The seventeenth century provoked numerous debates on what Marx, two hundred years later, referred to as the 'women question' (see Christopher Hill, *The World Turned Upside Down*). Few of these debates were satisfactorily resolved. They continued throughout the eighteenth and nineteenth centuries inspiring numerous essays, pamphlets, and tracts, including Mary Wollstonecraft's *A Vindication of the Rights of Women* (1792) and John Stuart Mill's *On the Subjection of Women* (1869), which became classics in their own time. Such works contributed to a growing body of opinion committed to the social emancipation of women through legal and political reform. By the end of the nineteenth century, women in most western societies had achieved a measure of formal equality, culminating in England at the turn of the century with the struggle for universal suffrage. Opportunities for higher education and professional employment followed and, particularly in matters concerning ownership of property and family relations, a greater degree of legal equality was formally introduced.

These limited reforms of the late nineteenth and early twentieth centuries were not radically improved in the decades between the two World Wars. Many of the inequalities described at the turn of the century by Charlotte Gilman (*Women and Economics*, USA 1898) and Olive Schreiner (*Women and Labour*, 1911) persisted and deepened as the Depression and massive unemployment encouraged more traditional attitudes to women as keepers of hearth and home. It was not until after the Second World War – during which many women became skilled in occupations and carried responsibilities normally associated with men – that the feminist movement re-emerged. Simone de Beauvoir's *The Second Sex* (France, 1949) set the scene for the explosion of polemical literature that followed in the sixties and seventies. The theme of female subordination in a culture dominated by male interests and sexual stereotypes taken up by Betty Freidan in *The Feminine Mystique* (1963), was articulated with increasing fervour in later works. Kate Millett's *Sexual Politics* (1969), Germaine Greer's *The Female Eunuch* (1970), Eva Figes' *Patriarchal Attitudes* (1970), Shulamith Firestone's *The Dialectic of Sex* (1970), Juliet Mitchell's *Woman's Estate* (1971), Sheila Rowbotham's *Woman's Consciousness, Man's World* (1973), and Jill Johnston's collection of essays *Lesbian Nation* (1973) are leading examples of contemporary analyses and feminist critiques. These and later feminist works, which in general have tended to focus upon more specific issues – e.g. rape (Susan Brownmiller, *Against Our Will*); prostitution (Kate Millett, *The Prostitution Papers*); housework (Ann Oakley, *Housewife*); female psychology (Juliet Mitchell, *Psychoanalysis and Feminism*) – examine the bases of sexual inequality in the historically specific context of advanced industrial societies. By comparison, Juliet Mitchell's earlier essay 'Women: The Longest Revolution' (*New Left Review* **40**, 1966) is one of the few attempts to analyse the bio-social structures that maintain women's subordination in a wider societal context. Her work has been followed by a number of theoretical developments, including Benston's 'The Political Economy of Women's Liberation' (*Monthly Review* **21**, 1969) and Szymanski's 'The Socialisation of Women's Oppression' (*Insurgent Sociologist* **VI**, 1976) as well as several historical studies of the causes of the present movement, notably Marlene Dixon's 'Why Women's Liberation?' (Dixon 1971), Jo Freeman's 'The Origins of the Women's Liberation Movement' (*American Journal of Sociology* 1973) and Maren Lockwood Carden's *The New Feminist Movement* (1974). However, the implications and consequences of the women's movement for the structure of industrial capitalism have yet to be fully worked out.

## 1. CLASSIC TEXTS OF FEMINISM

*1750–1900*

BEBEL, AUGUST *Woman in the Past, Present and Future* (trans. H.B. Adams Walther) London, 1885.

GILMAN, CHARLOTTE *Women and Economics* (Boston, 1898; reprinted by Harper and Row, New York, 1966).

MILL, JOHN STUART *On the Subjection of Women* (London, 1869; reprinted by Dent, London, 1970).

RADCLIFFE, MARY ANNE *The Female Advocate* (London, 1792).

WAKEFIELD, PRISCILLA *Reflections on the Present Condition of the Female Sex* (London, 1798).

WOLLSTONECRAFT, MARY *A Vindication of the Rights of Women* (London, 1792; reprinted by Dent, London, 1970).

*1900–1945*

GOLDMANN, EMMA *The Traffic in Women and Other Essays on Feminism* (Times Change Press, New York State, 1970); and 'The Tragedy of Woman's Emancipation' in

*Red Emma Speaks* A.K. Shulman (ed.) (Vintage Books, New York, 1972).

KENNIE, ANNIE *Memories of a Militant* (London, 1924).

LENIN, V.I. *On the Emancipation of Women* (Progress Publishers, Moscow, 1965).

SANGER, MARGARET *An Autobiography* (Dover Publications, New York, 1971). First published in 1938, the autobiography of one of the pioneers of the family planning movement in the United States.

STOPES, MARIE *Married Love* (Hogarth Press, London, 1918).

— *A New Gospel to all Peoples* (Putnams, London, 1920).

SCHREINER, OLIVE *Women and Labour* (London, 1911; reprinted by Virago, London, 1977).

TROTSKY, LEON *Women and the Family* (Pathfinder Press, New York, 1970).

In addition, edited selections of classic feminist writings are collected in *The Feminist Papers* Alice Rossi (ed.) (Columbia University Press, New York, 1973), and *Feminism: The Essential Historical Writings* Miriam Schneir (ed.) (Vintage Books, New York, 1972).

*1945 – the present*

ATKINSON, TI-GRACE  *Amazon Odyssey* (Links Books, New York, 1974).

DE BEAUVOIR, SIMONE *The Second Sex* (Gallimard, Paris, 1949). See also the comments on this work in the fourth volume of the author's autobiography, *All Said and Done* (Weidenfeld and Nicolson, London, 1972) in which she claims her analysis should have a 'much more materialistic emphasis'.

BIRD, C. and BRILLER, S. *Born Female: The High Cost of Keeping Women Down* (David and McKay, New York, 1968).

COSTA, M. D. *Women and the Subversion of the Community* (The Falling Wall Press, Bristol, 1972).

FIGES, EVA *Patriarchal Attitudes* (Faber and Faber, London, 1970).

FIRESTONE, SHULAMITH *The Dialectic of Sex: The Case for Feminist Revolution* (Morrow, New York, 1970).

FIRESTONE, S. and KOEDT, ANNE (eds) *Notes from the Second Year: Readings from the Women's Liberation Movement* (Old Chelsea Station Notes, New York, 1970).

FREIDAN, BETTY *The Feminine Mystique* (Norton, New York, 1963).

— *It Changed My Life: Writings on the Women's Movement* (Random House, New York, 1976). This collection of short essays includes an interesting exchange between Freidan and Simone de Beauvoir which illustrates some of the tensions between pragmatic and theoretical currents in the women's movement.

GASKOF, M.H. (ed.) *Roles Women Play : Readings Towards Women's Liberation* (Brooks Cole, Belmont, California, 1971).

GLAZER-MALBIN, N. and WAEHRER, (eds) *Women in a Man Made World* (Rand McNally, Chicago, 1972).

GORNICK, V. and MORAN, B. (eds) *Women in Sexist Society* (Basic Books, New York, 1971).

GREER, GERMAINE, *The Female Eunuch* (Macgibbon and Kee, London, 1970; McGraw Hill, New York, 1971).

GUETTEL, CHARNIE *Marxism and Feminism* (Hunter Rose Co., Toronto, 1974).

HEILBRUN, C. *Towards a Recognition of Androgyny* (Knopf, New York, 1973).

HERSCHBERGER, R. *Adam's Rib* (Pellegrini and Cudahy, New York, 1948).

JAMES, SELMA *A Woman's Place* (New York, 1953; reprinted by The Falling Wall Press, Bristol, 1972).

## 6 Work on Women

JOHNSTON, JILL *Marmalade Me* (Simon and Schuster, New York, 1971).

— *Lesbian Nation* (Simon and Schuster, New York, 1973). The essays collected in these volumes, most of which originally appeared in New York's *The Village Voice*, argue that lesbianism is the only solution to female oppression. 'Lois Lane is a Lesbian', which appears in *Marmalade Me*, has become particularly influential amongst some sections of the women's movement.

KOEDT, A., LEVINE, E. and RAPONE, A. (eds.) *Radical Feminism* (Quadrangle Books, New York, 1973).

MILLETT, KATE *Sexual Politics* (Equinox Books, New York, 1969 and Virago, London, 1978).

— *The Prostitution Papers* (Basic Books, New York, 1971 and Paladin, London, 1975).

— *Flying* (Basic Books, New York, 1974 and Hart Davis, London, 1975).

— *Sita* (Random House, New York, 1976 and Virago, London, 1977).

MITCHELL, JULIET *Woman's Estate* (Penguin, Harmondsworth, 1971).

MORGAN, ROBIN (ed.) *Sisterhood is Powerful* (Vintage Books, New York, 1970).

ROSZAK, B. and ROSZAK, T. (eds.) *Masculine, Feminine* (Harper and Row, New York, 1969).

ROSSI, ALICE Equality between the Sexes: An Immodest Proposal (*Daedalus* **93**, Spring 1964: 607-652).

ROWBOTHAM, SHEILA *Woman's Consciousness, Man's World* (Penguin, Harmondsworth, 1973).

— *Hidden from History* (Pluto, London, 1973).

SOLANAS, VALERIE *S.C.U.M. Manifesto* (Olympia Press, New York, 1968).

WANDOR, MICHELENE (ed.) *The Body Politic: Writings from the Women's Liberation Movement in Britain, 1969–1972* (Stage One Publications, London, 1972).

2. HISTORICAL ACCOUNTS OF FEMINISM AND THE
WOMEN'S MOVEMENT

BANKS, J. and O. *Feminism and Family Planning in Victorian England* (Schocken, London, 1972). See also, J. and O. Banks, Feminism and Social Change: A Case Study of a Social Movement, in *Explorations in Social Change* Zollschen, G. and Hirsch, W. (eds.) (Routledge and Kegan Paul, London, 1964).

BERG, B. *The Remembered Gate : Origins of American Feminism* 1800–1860 (Oxford University Press, London and New York, 1977).

CHAFE, W. *The American Woman: Her Changing Social, Economic and Political Roles, 1920–70* (Oxford University Press, New York, 1972).

EVANS, R. *The Feminist Movement in Germany, 1894–1933* (Sage, London, 1976).

HALL, R. *Marie Stopes* (Andre Deutsch, London, 1977).

HILL, CHRISTOPHER *The World Turned Upside Down* (Temple Smith, London, 1972). See in particular Chapter 15.

KAMM, J. *How Different from Us : A Biography of Miss Buss and Miss Beale* (Bodley Head, London, 1958).

LIDDINGTON, J. and NORRIS, J. *One Hand Tied Behind Us : The Rise of the Women's Suffrage Movement* (Virago, London, 1978).

MANTON, J. *Elizabeth Garrett Anderson* (Methuen, London, 1965).

MOBERLEY HILL, E. *Octavia Hill* (Constable, London, 1942).

O'NEILL, W. *Everyone was Brave: The Rise and Fall of Feminism in America* (Quadrangle Books, Chicago, 1969).

PANKHURST, SYLVIA *The Suffragette Movement* (1932; reprinted by Virago, London, 1977).

PUGH, M. Politicians and the Women's Vote (*History* **59**,

## 8   Work on Women

October 1974). An account of reactions of British politicians to the Suffragette Movement.

ROSE, C. *The Story of the Women's Movement in Ireland* (Arlen House, Galway, 1975).

ROSEN, A. *Rise Up Women: The Militant Campaign of the Women's Social and Political Union, 1903–1914* (Routledge and Kegan Paul, London, 1974).

SCOTT, A.F. and A.M. *One Half the People: The Fight for Women's Suffrage* (J.B. Linnicott, Philadelphia, 1974).

STITES, R. *The Women's Liberation Movement in Russia 1860–1930* (Princeton University Press, Princeton, 1978).

STRACHEY, R. *The Cause: A Short History of the Women's Movement* (1928; reprinted by Virago, London, 1977).

TAYLOR, L. The Unfinished Sexual Revolution (*Journal of Biosocial Science*, No. 3, 1971.) An insightful sociological account of the work of Marie Stopes.

THOMAS, K. Women in the Civil War Sects (*Past and Present*, **13**, 1958).

THONNERSON, W. *The Emancipation of Women: The Rise and Decline of the Women's Movement in German Social Democracy, 1863–1933* (Pluto, London, 1969).

TOMALIN, C. *The Life and Death of Mary Wollstonecraft* (Weidenfeld and Nicolson, London, 1974 and New Amercian Library, New York, 1974) There is a useful discussion of this book and the issues it raises concerning eighteenth and nineteenth century feminism by Ellen Moers in the *New York Review of Books* **XXIII**, No. 2, February 19, 1976.

The following deal specifically with the revival of feminism and the origins of the Women's Liberation Movement in the 1960s and 70s:

CARDEN, M.L. *The New Feminist Movement* (Russell Sage, New York, 1974).

DIXON, M. Why Women's Liberation?, in *Roles Women*

*Play: Readings Towards Women's Liberation* M. Gaskof (ed.) (Brooks Cole Publishing Co., California, 1971.

— Public Ideology and the Class Composition of Women's Liberation (*Berkeley Journal of Sociology*, **XVI**, 1971–2).

FREEMAN, J. The Origins of the Women's Liberation Movement (*American Journal of Sociology* **78**, 1973).

HOLE, J. and LEVINE, E. *The Rebirth of Feminism* (Quadrangle Books, New York, 1971).

HUNT, J. Women and Liberation (*Marxism Today*, November 1975).

KNUDSEN, D. The Declining Status of Women – Popular Myths and the Failure of Functionalist Thought (*Social Forces* **48**, 1969).

MAGAS, B. Theories of Women's Liberation (*New Left Review*, No. 66, 1971).

POLK, B. Women's Liberation: Movement for Equality, in *Toward a Sociology of Women* C. Safilios-Rothschild (ed.) (Xerox College Publishing, Lexington, Mass., 1972).

ROSSI, A. Sex Equality: the Beginnings of Ideology (*The Humanist* **28-29**, 1969).

3. THE POLITICAL ECONOMY OF SEXISM:
   THEORETICAL ORIENTATIONS

Although there has been extensive documentation of the persistence of sexual inequalities in economic, political, and social life, theoretical interpretations of the structural basis of sexism have remained relatively undeveloped. The increasing participation of women in the labour force has, however, shifted attention away from simple psycho-biological explanations towards more complex materialist analyses of the class position of women in capitalist society. Most of the items in this section take this as their theme in examining the relationship between sexual oppression and the political economy of industrial capitalism.

## 10    Work on Women

ALLEN, S. and BARKER, D. Sexual Divisions in Society, in *Sexual Divisions in Society: Process and Change* D. Barker and S. Allen (eds.) (Tavistock, London, 1976).

ADAMSON, O., BROWN, C., HARRISON, J., and PRICE, J. Women's Oppression under Capitalism (*Revolutionary Communist*, No.5, 1976).

BENSTON, M. The Political Economy of Women's Liberation (*Monthly Review* 21, September 1969).

CHRISTOFFEL, T. and KAUFFER, K. The Political Economy of Male Chauvinism, in *Up Against the American Myth* T. Christoffel (ed.) (Holt, Reinhart and Winston, New York, 1970).

DAVIES, M. and REICH, M. The Relationship between Sexism and Capitalism, in *The Capitalist System* R. Edwards (ed.) (Prentice Hall, Englewood Cliffs, 1972).

DELPHY, C. The Main Enemy: A Materialist Analysis of Women's Oppression (Women's Research and Resources Centre, *Explorations in Feminism*, No. 3, London, 1977).

EISENSTEIN, Z.R. (ed.) *Capitalist Patriachy and the case for Socialist Feminism* (Monthly Review Press, New York and London, 1979).

ENGELS, F. *The Origin of the Family, Private Property and the State* (Progress Publishers, Moscow, 1970).

GRABINER, E.V. and COOPER, L.B. Towards a Theoretical Orientation for Understanding Sexism (*Insurgent Sociologist*, 4, Fall 1973).

GOLDBERG, M. The Economic Exploitation of Women (*Review of Radical Political Economics* 2, Spring 1970).

HACKER, H. Women as a Minority Group (*Social Forces*, 30, 1951).

HAMILTON, R. *The Liberation of Women* (Allen and Unwin, London, 1978).

KUHN, A. and WOLPE, A. M. (eds.) *Feminism and Materialism* (Routledge and Kegan Paul, London, 1978).

MIDDLETON, C. Sexual Inequality and Stratification, in *The*

*Social Analysis of Class Structure* F. Parkin (ed.) (Tavistock, London, 1974).

MITCHELL, J. Women: The Longest Revolution *(New Left Review,* **40**, 1966).

REED, E. *Problems of Women's Liberation* (Pathfinder Press, New York, 1972).

ROWNTREE, M. and J. More on the Economy of Women's Liberation *(Monthly Review* **21**, January 1970).

SCHARF, B. Sexual Stratification and Social Stratification *(British Journal of Sociology* **28**, (4) 1977).

SZYMANSKI, A. The Socialisation of Women's Oppression: A Marxist Theory of the Changing Position of Women in Advanced Capitalist Society *(Insurgent Sociologist* **VI** (2) 1976).

## 4. FEMINIST CRITIQUES OF ACADEMIC SOCIAL SCIENCE

ACKER, J. Women and Social Stratification: A Case of Intellectual Sexism *(American Journal of Sociology* **78** (4) 1973).

BART, P. Sexism and Social Science *(Journal of Marriage and the Family* **33**, 1971).

BRIDENTHAL, R. and COONZ, C. (eds.) *Becoming Visible* (Houghton Mifflin, New York, 1977).

CARROLL, B. (ed.) *Liberating Women's History: Theoretical and Critical Essays* (University of Illinois Press, Urbana, 1976).

FRANKENBERG, R. 'In the Production of their Lives . . .', in *Sexual Divisions in Society: Process and Change* D. Barker and S. Allen (eds) (Tavistock, London, 1976).

MATHIEU, N. *Ignored by Some, Denied by Others* (Women's Research and Resources Centre, London, 1977).

MILLMAN, M. and KANTER, M. (eds.) *Another Voice: Femin-*

*ist Perspectives on Social Life and Social Science* (Double-day, Garden City, New York, 1975).

SAFILIOS-ROTHSCHILD, C. (ed.) *Towards a Sociology of Women* (Xerox College Publishing, Lexington, Mass., 1972).

# Domestic life and labour

Until recently domestic labour rarely featured in discussions of the home and family life. Those studies, such as Dennis, Henriques, and Slaughter's *Coal is Our Life* (Eyre and Spottiswoode, London, 1956) and Lee Rainwater's *Working Man's Wife* (Oceana Publications, New York, 1959) that dwelt on such matters, were primarily concerned with the demands of male employment upon the organization of household tasks. In most studies, however, women's activities in the home – cleaning, cooking, child-minding, shopping, mending, etc. – were neglected as apparently too familiar or insignificent to mention at all.

In the last few years domestic life and labour have become important areas of research and debate. Three related issues have attracted the attention of feminists and scholars alike: the economic status of housework, the social role of the housewife, and domestic relations between husbands and wives. Each of these issues stems from the increasing 'nuclearization' of the family and, in particular, the structural separation of work – economically productive labour – from family life. This tendency has transformed the economic significance of the family and domestic work. Whereas in traditional and early industrial societies women's domestic activities made a direct and independent contribution to economic life, as these activities became absorbed into specialized areas of production and paid work, the housewife became increasingly dependent upon commodity production and the wage labour of men. The structural consequences of this development are examined in Edward Shorter's *The Making of the Modern Family* (Basic Books, New York, 1975). The following discuss the family and domestic life in former times:

LASLETT, P. *The World We Have Lost* (rev. ed. Methuen, London, 1971).

LASLETT, P. with WALL, R. (eds.) *Household and Family in Past Time* (Cambridge University Press, Cambridge, 1972).

LERNER, G. *The Woman in American History* (Addison Wesley, Menlo Park, California, 1971).

STONE, L. The Rise of the Nuclear Family in Early Modern England, in *The Family in History* C. Rosenberg (ed.) (University of Philidelphia Press, 1975).

For further references, see:

MILDEN, J.W. *The Family in Past Time: A Guide to the Literature* (Garland Publishing, N.Y. 1977).

Although the importance of the household as a unit of production has declined with the expansion of industrial capitalism, the family continues to provide numerous personal and domestic services necessary for the reproduction, socialization, and maintenance of the labour force. The burden of such tasks falls mainly upon women in the home. However, because household labour is not calculated as paid work, its contribution to the economy is typically undervalued or ignored. Attempts to estimate the time spent on housework and its value to the economy are considered by the following:

BRODY, W.H. The Economic Value of a Housewife (*Research and Statistics Note*, No. 9, 1975).

CLARK, C. The Economics of Housework (*Institute of Statistics Bulletin* **20**, 1958).

GAUGER, W.H. Household Work: Can we add it to the GNP? (*Journal of Home Economics* **65** (7) 1973).

VANEK, J. Time Spent in Housework (*Scientific American* **231** (5) 1974).

Estimates of the monetary value of housework raise wider questions about the nature of domestic labour in relation to the economic order of industrial capitalism. Although feminists agree upon the economic value of unpaid domestic work, a major theoretical debate surrounds the question of whether housework is in the strict Marxian sense 'productive' or 'unproductive' work. For instance, Secombe (1973) argues that since domestic labour does not relate directly either to the process of production or the process of market exchange, the housewife does not produce 'surplus value' and consequently is not exploited in the same sense as wage labour, since the results of her efforts are rewarded and consumed within the home. In contrast, Dalla Costa and James (1972) claim housework is a form of productive labour in that through child-rearing it reproduces the supply of labour as well as daily maintaining the labour power of those who work for a wage. Finally, others (e.g. Gerstein, and Vogel) argue that the categories of 'productive' and 'unproductive' labour are wholly irrelevant to the analysis of housework which constitutes a special economic category of its own. Despite these theoretical differences, it is generally agreed that domestic labour is an integral and necessary part of the capitalist economy and the social relations of work. For a review of these issues, see Nona Glazer-Malbin, 'Housework' (*Signs* **1** (4) 1976) and also the following:

BENSTON, M. The Political Economy of Women's Liberation (*Monthly Review* **21** (4) 1969).

BROWN, B. The Natural and Social Division of Labour:

## 16　Work on Women

Engels and the Domestic Labour Debate (*M/F*, **1** (1) 1978).

COULSON, M., MAGAS, B. and WAINWRIGHT, H. The Housewife and her Labour under Capitalism: A Critique (*New Left Review* **89**, 1975).

CUVILLIER, R. The Housewife: An Unjustified Financial Burden on the Community (*Journal of Social Policy* **8**, part I. January 1979).

DALLA COSTA, M. and JAMES, S. *The Power of Women and the Subversion of the Community* (The Falling Wall Press, Bristol, 1972).

FEE, T. Domestic Labour: An Analysis of Housework and its Relation to the Production Process (*The Review of Radical Political Economics* **8** (1) 1976).

GARDINER, J. Women's Domestic Labour (*New Left Review* **89**, 1975).

— The Political Economy of Domestic Labour in Capitalist Society, in *Dependence and Exploitation in Work and Marriage* D. Barker and S. Allen, (eds) (Longman, Harlow, 1976).

GARDINER, J., HIMMELWEIT, S. and MACKINTOSH, M. Women's Domestic Labour (*Bulletin of the Conference of Socialist Economists* **IV** (2) 1975).

GERSTEIN, I. Domestic Work and Capitalism (*Radical America* **7**, July–October, 1973).

HARRISON, J. The Political Economy of Housework (*Bulletin of the Conference of Socialist Economists* **III**, 1974).

HIMMELWEIT, S. and MOHUN, S. Domestic Labour and Capital (*Cambridge Journal of Economics* **1** (1) 1977).

LANDES, J. Wages for Housework: Subsidising Capitalism? (*Quest*, Fall, 1975).

LERGUIA, I. and DUMOULIN, J. Toward a Science of Women' Liberation (*Political Affairs* **LI** (6 & 8) 1972).

SECOMBE, W. The Housewife and her Labour under Capitalism (*New Left Review* **83**, 1973).

SMITH, D. Women, the Family and Corporate Capitalism (*Berkeley Journal of Sociology* **XX**, 1975–6).

SZYMANSKI, A. The Socialisation of Women's Oppression: A Marxist Theory of the Changing Position of Women in Advanced Capitalist Society (*The Insurgent Sociologist* **VI** (2) 1976).

VOGEL, L. The Earthly Family (*Radical America* **7**, July–October, 1973).

WILLIS, E. Consumerism and Women (*Socialist Revolution* **3**, May–June, 1970).

Since Helena Lopata's early work on American housewives in the 1950s, several studies have examined housework as a social role. Socio-economic variations in the conception and performance of this role and its development through the life cycle of mothers and wives, are discussed in the following :

DAVIDOFF, L. The Rationalisation of Housework, in D. Barker and S. Allen (eds.) *Dependence and Exploitation in Work and Marriage* (Longman, Harlow, 1976).

GAIL, S. The Housewife, in R. Frazer (ed.), *Work : Twenty Personal Accounts* (Penguin, Harmondsworth, 1968).

GAVRON, H. *The Captive Wife* (Routledge and Kegan Paul, London, 1966).

HOBSON, D. Housewives : Isolation as Oppression, in The Women's Studies Group, Centre for Contemporary Cultural Studies, University of Birmingham (eds.) *Women Take Issue* (Hutchinson, London, 1978).

LOPATA, H. *Occupation: Housewife* (Oxford University Press, New York, 1971).

— *Widowhood in an American City* (Schenkman, Cambridge, Mass., 1973).

OAKLEY, A. *Housewife* (Allen Lane, London, 1974).

—*The Sociology of Housework* (Martin Robertson, London, 1974 and Pantheon, New York, 1974).

RAINWATER, L., COLEMAN, R. and HANDEL, G. *Working*

*Man's Wife* (Oceana Publications, New York, 1959).

SCOTT, J., and TILLY, L. Women's Work and Family in Nineteenth Century Europe (*Comparative Studies in Society and History*, January 1975).

SPRING-RICE, M. *Working Class Wives* (Pelican, Harmondsworth, 1939).

The increasing participation of married women in the labour force has far reaching implications for women's perceptions of their role and the relationship between husbands and wives. These and related issues are discussed in :

BERNARD, J. *The Future of Marriage* (Penguin, Harmondsworth, 1976).

BAUM, M. Love, Marriage and the Division of Labour, in P. Dreitzel (ed.), *Family, Marriage and the Struggle of the Sexes* (Macmillan, London and New York, 1972).

BELL, C. and NEWBY, H. Husbands and Wives: The Dynamics of the Deferential Dialectic, in D. Barker and S. Allen (eds.), *Dependence and Exploitation in Work and Marriage* (Longman, Harlow, 1976).

BOTT, E. and TOOMEY, D. Conjugal Roles and Social Networks in an Urban Working Class Sample (*Human Relations*, **24** (5) 1971).

COMER, L. *Wedlocked Women* (Feminist Books, Leeds, 1974).

DAVIDOFF, L., L'ESPERANCE, J. and NEWBY, H. Landscape with Figures: Home and Community in English Society, in A. Oakley and J. Mitchell (eds.), *The Rights and Wrongs of Women* (Penguin, Harmondsworth, 1976).

DELPHY, C. Continuities and Discontinuities in Marriage and Divorce, in D. Barker and S. Allen (eds.), *Sexual Divisions and Society, Process and Change* (Tavistock, London, 1976).

FOGARTY, M., RAPOPORT, R. and RAPOPORT, R. *Sex Career and Family* (Allen and Unwin, London, 1971).

GILLESPIE D. Who has the Power? The Marital Struggle, in P. Dreitzel (ed.), *Family, Marriage and the Struggle of the Sexes* (Macmillan, London and New York, 1972).

GOODE, W. The Theoretical Importance of Love (*American Sociological Review* **24**, 1959).

— *Women in Divorce* (The Free Press, New York, 1956).

KOMAROVSKY, M. *Blue Collar Marriage* (Random House, New York, 1964).

MARCEAU, J. Marriage, Role Division and Social Cohesion, in D. Barker and S. Allen (eds.), *Dependence and Exploitation in Work and Marriage* (Longman, Harlow, 1976).

MARSH, D. *Mothers Alone*, (Allen Lane, London, 1969).

PARSONS, T. Age and Sex in the Social Structure of the United States (*American Sociological Review* **7**, 1942).

TROTSKY, L. *Women and the Family* (Pathfinder Press, New York, 1970).

YOUNG, M. and WILLMOTT, P. *The Symmetrical Family: A Study of Work and Leisure in the London Region* (Routledge and Kegan Paul, London, 1973).

ZARETSKY, E. Capitalism, the Family and Personal Life (*Socialist Revolution*, Nos. 13/14 and 15, Jan–June 1973).

# Women and paid work

Women have always played an important, if under-stated role in economic life. In traditional and early industrial societies women commonly worked within household units – mainly as servants and agricultural labourers – where their labour constituted a fundamental part of the domestic economy. Industrialization increased women's opportunities for paid employment outside the home. Many were among the first factory workers, particularly in the textile industry where skills acquired in the home were easily transferred to larger units of production (see Neil Smelser, *Social Change in the Industrial Revolution: An Application of Theory to the Lancashire Cotton Industry, 1770–1840*, Routledge and Kegan Paul, London, 1959). The wider effects of industrialization on labour and employment are discussed by E.P. Thompson, *The Making of the English Working Class* (Gollancz, London, 1963) and E.J. Hobsbawm, *Industry and Empire* (Weidenfeld and Nicolson, London, 1968), but as yet there is no history of female labour that compares, for instance, with Hobsbawm's *Labouring Men* (Weidenfeld and Nicolson, London, 1968). For the most part, the contribution of women to the formation of industrial capitalism has been largely ignored. Ivy Pinchbeck's pioneering study, *Women Workers and the Industrial Revolution* (1930) remains a classic in what was until recently a relatively unexplored field:

ALEXANDER, S. Women's Work in Nineteenth Century London: A Study in the Years 1820–1850, in A. Oakley and J. Mitchell (eds.), *The Rights and Wrongs of Women* (Penguin, Harmondsworth, 1976).

CLARK, A. *The Working Life of Women in the Seventeenth Century* (1919; republished by Cass, London, 1968).

COTT, N. *The Bonds of Womanhood: Women's Sphere in New England, 1780–1835* (Yale University Press, New Haven, 1977).

CROW, D. *The Victorian Woman* (Allen and Unwin, London, 1971).

DAVIES, M.L. (ed.) *Life as We have known It* (1931; republished by Virago, London, 1975).

FREDEMAN, W. Emily Faithfull and the Victorian Press (*The Library* **XXIV** (2) June 1974).

HEWITT, M. *Wives and Mothers in Victorian Industry* (Barrie and Rockliff, London, 1958).

HOLCOME, LEE *Victorian Ladies at Work: Middle Class Working Women in England and Wales, 1850–1914* (David and Charles, Newton Abbot, 1973).

NEFF, W. *Victorian Working Women: A Historical and Literary Study of Women in British Industries and Professions, 1832–1850* (Columbia University Press, New York, 1929).

PINCHBECK, I. *Women Workers and the Industrial Revolution* (Oxford University Press, London, 1930).

RICHARDS, E. Women in the British Economy since 1700 (*History* **59** (197) October 1974).

SHORTER, E. Women's Work: What Difference did Capitalism Make? (*Theory and Society* **3** (4) Winter 1976).

SMUTS, R.W. *Women and Work in America* (Schocken Books, New York, 1971).

VICINUS, M. (ed.) *Suffer and Be Still: Women in the Victorian Age* (Indiana University Press, Bloomington, 1972).

WERTHEIMER, B., *We Were There: The Story of Working Women in America* (Pantheon Books, New York, 1971).

It is clear from Richards's and Pinchbeck's accounts that during the industrial revolution women earned considerably less than men in similar work ; furthermore, they were often excluded from opportunities to acquire newly developing marketable skills. These inequalities in the rewards and conditions of employment persist to the present day. Although women are now an increasingly large proportion of the labour force of industrial societies (approximately 40 per cent in Britain and the United States), they are still concentrated within the lower paid, least prestigious and influential areas of work. As the following suggest, the sex typing of occupations and the traditionally low status of women combine to make this pattern difficult to break :

BARRON, R.D. and NORRIS, G.M. Sexual Divisions and the Dual Labour Market, in D. Barker and S. Allen (eds.), *Dependence and Exploitation in Work and Marriage* (Longman, Harlow, 1976).

BASS, B., KRUSELL, J. and ALEXANDER, R. Male Managers' Attitudes towards Working Women (*American Behavioural Scientist* 15, Nov–Dec 1971).

BECKER, G.S. *The Economics of Discrimination* (The University of Chicago Press, Chicago, 1971).

BEECHEY, V. Some Notes on Female Wage Labour in Capitalist Production (*Capital and Class*, No. 3, 1977).

BLAXALL, M. and REAGAN, B. *Women and the Work Place: The Implications of Occupational Segregation* (The University of Chicago Press, Chicago, 1976).

BROWN, R. Women as Employees: Some Comments on Research in Industrial Sociology, in D. Barker and S. Allen (eds.), *Dependence and Exploitation in Work and Marriage* (Longman, Harlow, 1976).

BROWNLEE, W. and BROWNLEE, M. (eds.) *Women in the American Economy* (Yale University Press, New Haven, 1976).

CHAPMAN, J.R. (ed.) *Economic Independence for Women: The*

*Foundation for Equal Rights* (Sage, London, 1976).

CHIPLIN, B. and SLOANE, P. Sexual Discrimination in the Labour Market (*British Journal of Industrial Relations* **XII** (3) 1974).

— *Sex Discrimination in the Labour Market* (Macmillan, London, 1978).

(Note : A useful review of this book by I. Bruegel appears in *M/F*, No. I, 1978).

COSER, R. and RUKOFF, G. Women in the Occupational World: Social Disruption and Conflict (*Social Problems* **18** (4) 1971).

GOLDBERG, M. The Economic Exploitation of Women (*Review of Radical Political Economics*) **2** (1) Spring 1970).

GRIMM, J.W. and STERN, R. Sex Roles and Internal Labour Market Structures: The Female Semi–Professions (*Social Problems* **21** (5) June 1974).

GROSS, E. Plus ca Change? The Sexual Structure of Occupations over Time (*Social Problems* **16** (2) Fall 1968).

GUILBERT, M. *Les Fonctions des Femmes dans l'Industrie* (Mouton et Cie, Paris, 1966).

KREPS, J. *Sex in the Market Place: American Women at Work* (Johns Hopkins, Baltimore, 1971).

KREPS, J.(ed.) *Women and the American Economy: A Look to the 1980s* (Prentice Hall, Englewood Cliffs, 1976).

LLOYD C. (ed.) *Sex, Discrimination and the Division of Labour* (Columbia University Press, New York, 1975).

MACKIE, L. and PATTULLO, P. *Women at Work* (Tavistock, London, 1977).

MADDEN, J.F. *The Economics of Sex Discrimination* (Lexington Books, Lexington, 1973).

OPPENHEIMER, V. The Sex Labelling of Jobs (*Industrial Relations* **7** May 1968).

— *The Female Labour Force in the United States* (Berkeley Institute of International Studies, Berkeley, 1970).

— Demographic Influence on Female Employment and the

Status of Women (*American Journal of Sociology* **78** (4) January, 1973).

SOCIAL PROBLEMS *Special Issue: Women and Work* **22** (4) April 1975.

One crucial aspect of women's experience of work is the tension between employment and family roles. These tensions – which most acutely affect working mothers – were analysed in the mid-fifties by Myrdal and Klein in their study, *Women's Two Roles*. Since then the number of married women in long-term employment has greatly increased, suggesting that despite the difficulties of reconciling work with domestic tasks, women enter and remain in employment partly from choice. Recent studies support this view but reveal continuing tensions between occupational roles and the demands of family life:

BERNARD, J. *Women, Wives and Mothers: Values and Options* (Aldine, Chicago, 1975).

CALLAHAN, S. *The Working Mother* (Macmillan, New York, 1971).

HEDGES, J. and BARNETT, J. Working Women and the Division of Household Tasks (*Monthly Labour Review* **95** (3) April 1972).

HOFFMAN, L. and NYE, F. (eds.) *The Employed Mother in America* (Rand McNally, Chicago, 1963).

— *Working Mothers* (Rand McNally, Chicago, 1973).

KLEIN, V. *Britain's Married Women Workers* (Routledge and Kegan Paul, London, 1965).

MYRDAL, A. and KLEIN, V. *Women's Two Roles* (Routledge and Kegan Paul, London, 1956).

WAITE, L.J. Working Wives: 1940–1960 (*American Sociological Review*, **41** (1) February 1976).

YUDKIN, S. and HOLME, A. *Working Mothers and their Children* (Michael Joseph, London, 1963).

This last section documents the difficulties and experiences of women in predominantly professional employment. Much of the literature draws on American material but some existing studies refer to the British case:

ANGEL, J.L. *Careers for Women in the Legal Profession* (New York World Trade Academy Press, New York, 1961).

ARCHIBALD, K. Women in Banking (*Banking*, July 1973).

ASTIN, H. *The Woman Doctorate in America: Origins, Careers and Family* (Russell Sage Foundation, New York, 1969).

BECK, E. The Female Clergy: A Case of Professional Marginality (*American Journal of Sociology* **72** March 1967).

BENET, M. *The Secretarial Ghetto* (McGraw Hill, New York, 1972).

BERNARD, J. *Academic Women* (The Pennsylvania State University Press, University Park, 1964).

BLACKSTONE, T. and FULTON, O. Sex Discrimination among University Teachers: A British–American Comparison (*British Journal of Sociology* **26** (3) 1975).

DAVIES, M. Woman's Place is at the Typewriter: the Feminisation of the Clerical Labour Force (*Radical America* **8** (4) July–August, 1974).

DONNISON, J. *Midwives and Medical Men: A History of Inter-Professional Rivalries and Women's Rights* (Heinemann, London, 1976).

ELSTON, M. Women in the Medical Profession: Whose Problem?, in M. Stacey (ed.), *Health Care and the Division of Labour* (Croom Helm, London, 1977).

EPSTEIN, C. *Woman's Place: Options and Limits in Professional Careers* (The University of California Press, Berkeley, 1970).

— Positive Effects of the Double Negative (*American Journal of Sociology* **78** (4) January 1973).

— Bringing Women in: Rewards, Punishments, and the Structure of Achievement (*Annals of the New York Academy of Sciences* **208** March 15 1973).

FAVA, S. The Status of Women in Professional Sociology (*American Sociological Review* **25** 1960).

## 26  Work on Women

FURNISS, W. and GRAHAM, P. (eds.) *Women in Higher Education* (American Council on Education, Washington, 1974).

GRAHAM, S. and LLEWELLYN, C. Women in Banking, Unpublished paper, available from the authors at Nuffield College, Oxford.

GRIFFIN, S. *Women in Top Financial Jobs* (Griffin, Oxford, 1973).

HOPE, E., KENNEDY, M. and DE WINTER, A. Homeworkers in North London, in D. Barker and S. Allen (eds.), *Dependence and Exploitation in Work and Marriage* (Longman, Harlow, 1976).

JEFFERYS, M. and ELLIOTT, P. *Women in Medicine: the Results of an Inquiry Conducted by the Medical Practioners Union in 1962–1963* (Office of Health Economics, London, 1966).

KANOWITZ, L. *Women and the Law* (The University of New Mexico Press, Albuquerque, 1967).

KANTER, R.M. *Men and Women of the Corporation* (Basic Books, New York, 1977).

LEWIN, A. and DUCHAN, L. Women in Academia (*Science*, 3 September 1971).

LOPATE, C. *Women in Medicine* (Johns Hopkins University Press, Baltimore, 1968).

MATTFELD, J. and AKEN, C. *Women and the Scientific Professions* (The M.I.T. Press, Cambridge, Massachusetts, 1965).

MITCHELL, M.B. The Status of Women in the American Psychological Association (*American Psychologist* **6** 1951).

PERUCCI, C. *Minority Status and the Pursuit of Professional Careers : Women in Science and Engineering* (Institute for the Study of Social Change, Purdue University, Working Paper No. 34, Lafayette, Indiana, 1970).

ROSSI, A. Barriers to the Career Choice of Engineering, Medicine or Science among American Women, in J.

Mattfeld and C. Aken (eds.), *Women and the Scientific Professions* (M.I.T. Press, Mass., 1965).

ROSSI, A. Women in Science, Why so Few? (*Science* **148**, (3674) May 28 1965).

ROSSI, A. and CALDERWOOD, A. (eds.) *Academic Women on the Move* (Russell Sage Foundation, New York, 1973).

RUINA, E. (ed.) *Women in Science and Technology* (The M.I.T. Press, Mass., 1974).

SCHILLER, A. Women in Librarianship, in, *Advances in Librarianship, Vol. 4* (The Academic Press, New York, 1974).

SIMON, R.J., CLARK, S., and GALWAY, K. The Woman Ph.D. (*Social Problems* **15** (2) Fall, 1967).

SMITH, R. Sex and Occupational Role on Fleet Street, in D. Barker and S. Allen (eds.), *Dependence and Exploitation in Work and Marriage* (Longman, Harlow, 1976).

TAVISTOCK INSTITUTE *Women in Top Jobs: An Interim Report* (Political and Economic Planning, London, 1967).

THEODORE, A. (ed.) *The Professional Woman* (Schenkman Publishing, Cambridge, Mass., 1971).

WHITE, M.S. Psychological and Social Barriers to Women in Science (*Science*, 23 October 1970).

WILLIAMS, J.J. Patients and Prejudice : Lay Attitudes Towards Women Physicians (*American Journal of Sociology* **51** 1946).

— The Woman Physician's Dilemma (*Journal of Social Issues* **6** 1950).

# Health, education, and welfare

The extension of state welfare and educational services over the last thirty years has probably improved the life chances of women as much as those of men. However, whilst few critics would oppose the principles behind these provisions, feminists and others have begun to examine the assumptions implicit in the distribution of these services to women. In general, it is argued there is a strong presumption in welfare and educational policies that women are economically dependent upon fathers or husbands and that their primary role is to become mothers and wives. Similar assumptions about the status and proclivities of women have been detected in the delivery of medical care. In particular, many studies have documented the moralistic and often alienating attitudes of the medical profession in dealing with female and specifically sexual complaints. It was largely in response to these practices that the Boston Women's Health Collective produced their excellent manual, *Our Bodies, Ourselves*, based on the radical assumption that in an age of professionals, the best experts on women are women themselves.

## HEALTH

The literature on women and medical care is vast. Much of it has been compiled in a recent bibliography by Sheryl Ruzek, *Women and Health Care* (Program on Women, Northwestern University, Evanston, Illinois, 1975) which should be used in conjunction with the following:

THE BOSTON WOMEN'S HEALTH BOOK COLLECTIVE *Our Bodies, Ourselves* (rev. ed., Simon and Schuster, New York, 1976; English ed. edited by A. Phillips and J. Rakusen, Penguin, Harmondsworth, 1978).

COOK, F. *The Plot Against the Patient* (Prentice Hall, Englewood Cliffs, 1967).

COREA, G. *Women's Health: The Hidden Malpractice* (Morrow, New York, 1977).

DELANEY, J., LUPTON, M. and TOTH, E. *The Curse: A Cultural History of Menstruation* (Dutton, New York, 1976).

EHRENREICH, B. and ENGLISH, D. *Witches, Midwives and Nurses: A History of Women Healers* (The Feminist Press, Old Westbury, N.Y., 1972).

— *Complaints and Disorders: The Sexual Politics of Sickness* (The Feminist Press, Old Westbury, N.Y., 1973).

FRANKFORT, E. *Vaginal Politics* (Quadrangle Books, New York, 1972).

FRYER, P. *The Birth Controllers* (Secker and Warburg, London, 1965).

GORDON, L. *Woman's Body, Woman's Right: A Social History of Birth Control in America* (Grossmann, New York, 1976).

GREENWOOD, V. and YOUNG, J. *Abortion on Demand* (Pluto Press, London, 1976).

HORDERN, A. *Legal Abortion: The English Experience* (The Pergamon Press, Oxford, 1971).

HOROBIN, G. (ed.) *Experience with Abortion* (Cambridge University Press, Cambridge, 1973).

LEESON, J. and GRAY, J. *Women and Medicine* (Tavistock, London, 1979).

LENNANE, J.K. and LENNANE, R.J. Alleged Psychogenic Disorders in Women: A Possible Manifestation of Sexual Prejudice (*New England Journal of Medicine* **228** (6) February 1973).

LUY, M. What's behind Women's Wrath towards Gynaecologists? (*Modern Medicine*, October 14, 1974).

NAVARRO, V. Women in Health Care (*New England Journal of Medicine* **292** (8) February, 1975).

OAKLEY, A. Wisewoman and Medicine Man: Changes in the Management of Childbirth, in A. Oakley and J. Mitchell (eds) *The Rights and Wrongs of Women* (Penguin Books, Harmondsworth, 1976).

PEEL, J. and POTTS, M. *Textbook of Contraceptive Practice* (Cambridge University Press, Cambridge, 1969).

ROSE, H. and HANMER, J. Women's Liberation, Reproduction and the Technological Fix, in D. Barker and S. Allen (eds) *Sexual Divisions and Society: Process and Change* (Tavistock, London, 1976).

SCOTT, C. *The World of a Gynaecologist* (Oliver and Boyd, London, 1968).

SCULLY, D. and BART, P. A Funny Thing happened on the Way to the Orifice: Women in Gynaecology Textbooks (*American Journal of Sociology* **78** (4) 1973).

SIMMS, M. Gynaecologists, Contraception and Abortion: From Birkett to Lane (*World Medicine* October 23, 1974).

SMITH, D.S. Family Limitation, Sexual Control and Domestic Feminism, in, L. Banner and M. Hartman (eds.), *Clio's Consciousness Raised* (Harper and Row, New York, 1974).

ZOLA, I.K. Medicine as an Institution of Social Control (*Sociological Review* **20** (4) 1970).

EDUCATION

Education has long been seen as one of the most important

channels of social mobility and sexual equality. However, although in the last thirty years opportunities for women to enter higher education have generally increased, men still outnumber women at universities and polytechnics by two to one (Department of Education and Science, *Statistics of Education*, vols. 3 and 6, HMSO, London, 1978). This pattern, which is replicated in most European countries, is not so much a consequence of formal institutional barriers as the subtle and pervasive process of sexual socialization which permeates all grades of education, conditioning and generally depressing the intellectual aspirations and attainments of girls. As Byrne amongst others suggests, the unwritten assumptions of this 'hidden curriculum' appear strongly resistant to educational innovation and organizational change:

BAKER, L. *The Seven Sisters and the Failure of Women's Education* (Macmillan, New York, 1976).

BLACKSTONE, T. The Education of Girls Today, in A. Oakley and J. Mitchell (eds.) *The Rights and Wrongs of Women* (Penguin, Harmondsworth, 1976).

BORING, P. Sex Stereotyping in Educational Guidance, in *Sex Role Stereotyping in the Schools* (National Educational Association, Washington, D.C., 1973).

BRIERLEY, J. Sex Differences in Education (*Trends in Education* February, 1975).

BRITTAIN, V. *Women at Oxford* (Harrap, London, 1960).

BYRNE, E. *Women and Education* (Tavistock, London, 1978).

DEEM, R. *Women and Schooling* (Routledge and Kegan Paul, London, 1978).

DEPARTMENT OF EDUCATION AND SCIENCE *Curricula Differences between the Sexes* (Education Survey 21, HMSO, London, 1975).

FRAZIER, N. and SADKER, M. *Sexism in Schools and Society* (Harper and Row, New York, 1973).

GRAHAM, P. Expansion and Exclusion: A History of Women

in American Higher Education, (*Signs* **3**, (4) Spring 1978).

KAMM, J. *How Different from Us: A Biography of Miss Buss and Miss Beale* (Methuen, London, 1958).

LEVY, B. Sex Role Socialisation in the Schools, in, *Sex Role Stereotyping in the Schools* (National Educational Association, Washington, D.C., 1973).

MARKS, P. Femininity in the Classroom: An Account of Changing Attitudes, in, A Oakley and J. Mitchell (eds.) *The Rights and Wrongs of Women* (Penguin, Harmondsworth, 1976).

NEWCOMER, M. *A Century of Higher Education for Women* (Harper and Row, New York, 1959).

OATES, M. and WILLIAMSON, S. Women's Colleges and Women Achievers (*Signs* **3** (4) Spring, 1978).

ROBY, P. Women and American Higher Education (*Annals of the American Academy of Political and Social Science* **404** 1972).

SHAW, J. Finishing School: Some Implications of Sex Segregated Education, in, D. Barker and S. Allen (eds.) *Sexual Divisions and Society: Process and Change* (Tavistock, London, 1976).

SHARPE, S. *Just Like a Girl* (Penguin, Harmondsworth, 1976).

SIGNS *Women, Science and Society* (Special Issue: **4** (1) Autumn 1978).

UNESCO *Women, Education, Equality: A Decade of Experiment* (UNESCO Press, Paris, 1975).

WOLPE, A. *Some Processes in Sexist Education* (Women's Research and Resources Centre, Explorations in Feminism, London, 1976).

WELFARE

Societal expectations of women are nowhere so clearly defined or shaped than in the ideology and provisions of the welfare state. As Wilson remarks, ' . . . the manipulations of the Welfare State offer a unique demonstration of how the State can prescribe what woman's consciousness should be' (*Women and the Welfare State*: p. 7). Above all, women are seen as Mothers – nuturant, submissive, passive, and socially dependent upon their husband's earnings. A fundamental part of this conception is the idea that a woman cannot be both married and at the same time independent. This general principle (which underlies most welfare policies in the West) is increasingly becoming empirically implausible and ideologically unacceptable, and is at the centre of both liberal and radical critiques:

FEAGIN, J.R. America's Welfare Stereotypes (*Social Science Quarterly* **52** (4) 1972).

GARDINER, J. Women and Unemployment (*Red Rag*, no.10, 1975); obtainable from, 22, Murray Mews, London N.W. 1).

GLASSMAN, C. Women and the Welfare System, in, R. Morgan (ed.) *Sisterhood is Powerful* (Vintage Books, New York, 1970).

HANMER, J. Community Action, Women's Aid and the Women's Liberation Movement, in M. May (ed.) *Women in the Community* (Routledge and Kegan Paul, London, 1976).

H. M. GOVERNMENT *Report of the Committee on One Parent Families* (Finer Report) Vols I and II, Cmnd. 5269 (HMSO, London, 1974).

IGLITZIN, L.B. A Case Study in Patriarchal Politics: Women on Welfare (*American Behavioural Scientist* **17** (4) March 1974).

LAND, H. Women, Work and Social Security (*Journal of Social and Economic Administration* **5** (3) 1971).

— The Myth of the Male Breadwinner (*New Society*, October 9, 1975).

— Women: Supporters or Supported?, in, D. Barker and S.

Allen (eds.) *Sexual Divisions and Society: Process and Change* (Tavistock, London, 1976).

— Sex Role Stereotyping in the Social Security and Income Tax Systems, in, J. Chetwynd and O. Hartnett (eds.) *The Sex Role System* (Routledge and Kegan Paul, London, 1978).

LISTER, R. *As Man and Wife?* (Child Poverty Action Group, Poverty Research Series 2, London, 1973).

MAYO, M. (ed.) *Women in the Community* (Routledge and Kegan Paul, London, 1976).

TOREN, N. *Social Work: The Case of a Semi-Profession* (Sage Publications, Beverley Hills, 1972).

WALTON, R.G. *Women in Social Work* (Routledge and Kegan Paul, London, 1975).

WILSON, E. *Women and the Welfare State* (Tavistock, London, 1977).

# Law and politics

The two major battles fought by nineteenth century feminists were for women's suffrage and equal treatment in law. In both cases, women eventually triumphed and were given the vote and a measure of legal equality. However, despite these gains women have yet to play a central role in political life and still suffer from judicial discrimination in courts. Recent legislation in Britain and the United States has recognized both the fact of discrimination and the potentially important role of the legal system in establishing women's rights (see Rendel 1978). Aspects of the legal status of women and their treatment before the law are considered in the following:

CHAPMAN, J. and GATES, M. (eds.) *Women into Wives: The Legal and Economic Aspect of Marriage* (Sage, London, 1977).

CHESNEY-LIND, M. Judicial Enforcement of the Female Sex Role: The Family Court and the Female Delinquent (*Issues in Criminology*, 8 (2) Fall 1973).

COOTE, A. Equality and the Curse of the Quango (*New Statesman*, December 1, 1978).

COOTE, A. and GILL, T. *Women's Rights: A Practical Guide* (Penguin, Harmondsworth, 1972).

COUSSINS, J. *The Equality Report* (National Council for Civil Liberties, Rights for Women Unit, London, 1976).

## 36 Work on Women

DECROW, K. *Sexist Justice* (Vintage Books, New York, 1974).

GARFINKEL, A., LEFCOURT, C. and SCHULDER, D. Women's Servitude under Law, in R. Lefcourt (ed.), *Law Against the People* (Vintage, New York, 1971).

GOODY, J. Inheritance, Property and Women: Some Comparative Considerations, in, J. Goody, J. Thirsk and E.P. Thompson (eds.), *Family and Inheritance* (Cambridge University Press, Cambridge, 1976).

HIBEY, R. The Trial of a Rape Case (*American Criminal Law Review*, 2 Part 2, 1973).

KANOWITZ, L. *Women and the Law: The Unfinished Revolution* (University of New Mexico Press, Albuquerque, 1969).

O'DONOVAN, K. The Male Appendage: Legal Definitions of Women, in S. Burman (ed.) *Fit Work for Women* (Croom Helm, London, 1979).

RENDEL, M. Legislating for Equal Pay and Opportunity for Women in Britain (*Signs* 3 (4) Summer 1978).

SACHS, A. The Myth of Male Protectiveness and the Legal Subordination of Women, in C. and B. Smart (eds.), *Women, Sexuality and Social Control* (Routledge and Kegan Paul, London, 1978).

SMITH, A. The Woman Offender, in L. Blom-Cooper (ed.), *Progress in Penal Reform* (Clarendon Press, Oxford, 1974).

A significant indicator – and a continuing cause – of the secondary status of women is the relatively minor part they play in the formal institutions of political life. Although many women contribute as voluntary workers to political parties (see Daniels *et al.* 1976), they are for the most part peripheral to decision-making processes and the centres of power. This is true not only of their position in legislative assemblies but also of their involvement in trade unions and labour organizations.

ANDERSON, K. Working Women and Political Participation (*American Journal of Political Science* **19** 1975).

BAXANDALL, R. Women and American Trade Unions: A Historical Analysis, in A. Oakley and J. Mitchell (eds.), *The Rights and Wrongs of Women* (Penguin, Harmondsworth, 1976).

BERQUIST, V. Women's Participation in Labour Organisations (*Monthly Labour Review*, October 1973).

BOALS, K. Women and Political Science: A Review Essay (*Signs* **1** (1) Autumn 1975).

BOURQUE, S.C. and GROSSHOLTZ, J. Politics is an Unnatural Practice: Political Science looks at Female Participation (*Politics and Society* **4** 1974).

COOK, A. Women in American Trade Unions (*Annals* **375** July 1968).

COSER, R. and EPSTEIN, C. (eds.) *Access to Power: Cross National Studies on Women and Elites* (Allen and Unwin, New York and London, 1979).

DANIELS, A.K., ERIKSSON-JOSLYN, K. and RUZEK, S. *Volunteerism in the Lives of Women* (The Program on Women, Northwestern University, Illinois, 1976).

DEWEY, L. Women in Labour Unions (*Monthly Labour Review* February 1971).

GITHENS, M. and PRESTAGE, J. (eds.) *A Portrait of Marginality* (David McKay, New York, 1977).

GOOT, M. and REID, S. and E. *Women and Voting Studies: Mindless Matrons or Sexist Scientism?* (Sage, London, 1975).

GREENSTEIN, F. Sex Related Political Differences in Childhood (*Journal of Politics* **23** 1961).

KIRKPATRICK, J. *Political Woman* (Basic Books, New York, 1974).

MAGAS, B. Sex Politics, Class Politics (*New Left Review* No. 66, March–April 1971).

McCOURT, K. *Working Class Women and Grass Root Politics* (Indiana University Press, Bloomington, 1977).

MILBURN, J.F. *Women as Citizens* (Sage, London, 1976).

MOORE, J. Patterns of Women's Participation in Voluntary Associations (*American Journal of Sociology*, **45** May 1961).

RAPHAEL, E. Working Women and their Membership in Labour Unions (*Monthly Labour Review*, May 1974).

ROWBOTHAM, S. *Hidden from History* (Pluto, London, 1973).

RUTGERS UNIVERSITY (Institute of Politics, Centre for the American Woman and Politics) *The Political Participation of Women in the United States, 1950–1976* (Scarecrow Press, Metuchen, New Jersey, 1978).

— *Voluntary Participation among Women in the United States: A Selected Bibliography 1950–1976* (Rutgers University, New Brunswick, 1976).

SHANLEY, M. and SCHUCK, V. In Search of Political Woman (*Social Science Quarterly* **55** 1975).

THOMPSON, D. Women and Nineteenth Century Radical Politics, in A. Oakley and J. Mitchell (eds.), *The Rights and Wrongs of Women* (Penguin, Harmondsworth, 1976).

VOLGY, T. and VOLGY, S. Women and Politics: Political Correlates of Sex Role Acceptance (*Social Science Quarterly*, **55** 1975).

WERTHEIMER, B. and NELSON, A. *Trade Union Women: A Study of their Participation in New York City Local* (Praeger, New York, 1975).

# Crime and deviance

Criminological theory and research has rarely been concerned with female offenders: indeed most studies of social deviance make no mention of women at all. Nonetheless, sex differences are at least significant as age, race, and socio-economic variables commonly used to explain the distribution and prevalence of crime. Paradoxically, the reason for this omission lies partly in the nature of the differences themselves. With the exception of shoplifting and soliciting, the number of female offenders is nowhere near as high as the number of male offenders known to the police (see R.J. Simon, *The Contemporary Woman and Crime*, National Institute of Mental Health, Maryland, 1975). Moreover, women commit mostly petty offences and seldom re-appear as repeat offenders in court. Thus, women pose relatively minor problems for agencies of social control, and have consequently attracted little attention in the literature on social deviance and criminal research.

As a result, knowledge of the character and causes of female deviance is still of modest dimensions. Most explanations have been based explicitly or implicitly upon variants of psycho-physiological determinism. For example, in a classic study, Lombroso argued that women are 'congenitally less inclined to crime' whilst claiming the female offender is a 'pathologically deviant type' (*The Female Offender*, 1895).

Similarly, in a much more recent study, Cowie, *et al.* attempt to explain the comparatively low incidence of female delinquency in terms of 'hereditary dispositions' and 'sex-linked genes', concluding that 'the female personality, more timid, more lacking in enterprise, may guard her against delinquency' (*Delinquency in Girls*, 1968:167). Others have appealed to emotional instability, the menopause, menstruation, and hormonal imbalance as the causes of female crime. See:

COWIE, J., COWIE, V. and SLATER, E. *Delinquency in Girls* (Heinemann, London, 1968).

KONOPKA, G. *The Adolescent Girl in Conflict* (Prentice Hall, Englewood Cliffs, 1966).

LOMBROSO, C. *The Female Offender* (Fisher Unwin, London, 1895).

POLLAK, O. *The Criminality of Women* (A.S. Barnes, New York, 1961).

SUVAL, E.M. and BRISSON, R.C. Neither Beauty nor Beast: Female Criminal Homicide Offenders (*International Journal of Criminology and Penology*, **2** (1) 1974).

THOMAS, W.I. *The Unadjusted Girl* (Harper and Row, New York, 1923).

VEDDER, C. *The Delinquent Girl* (Thomas, Springfield, 1970).

WISE, N. Juvenile Delinquency among Middle Class Girls, in E. Vaz (ed.), *Middle Class Juvenile Delinquency* (Harper and Row, New York, 1967).

Many of the assumptions underlying psycho-biological explanations are critically examined in the following:

ADLER, F. *Sisters in Crime: The Rise of the New Female Criminal* (McGraw Hill, New York, 1975).

HEIDENSOHN, F. The Deviance of Women (*British Journal of Sociology* **19** (2) 1968).

— Sex, Crime and Society, in G. Harrison and J. Perl (eds.),
    *Biosocial Aspects of Sex* (Blackwell, Oxford, 1970).

HOFFMAN-BUSTAMANTE, D. The Nature of Female Crim-
    inality *(Issues in Criminology* **8** (2) 1973).

KLEIN, D. The Etiology of Female Crime: A Review of the
    Literature *(Issues in Criminology* **8** (2) 1973).

KLEIN, D. and KRESS, J. Any Woman Blues: A Critical
    Over-view of Women, Crime and the Criminal Justice
    System *(Crime and Social Justice* Spring/Summer 1976).

MILLMAN, M. She Did it All for Love: A Feminist View of
    the Sociology of Deviance, in M. Millman and R.M.
    Kanter (eds.), *Another Voice: Feminist Perspectives on
    Social Life and Social Science* (Anchor Books, New York,
    1975).

ROSENBLUM, K.E. Female Deviance and the Female Sex
    Role: A Preliminary Investigation *(British Journal of
    Sociology* **26** (2) 1975).

SMART, C. *Women, Crime and Criminology* (Routledge and
    Kegan Paul, London, 1976).

SMART, C. and B. (eds.) *Women, Sexuality and Social Control*
    (Routledge and Kegan Paul, London, 1978).

One of the more interesting hypotheses advanced to explain
the declining sex ratio in crimes since the early sixties suggests that as women achieve greater equality in other areas, so
they become more equal in crime (cf. Adler, *Sisters in Crime*).
Similarly, with the movement towards equality, feminists
have shown a greater interest in acts of deviance in which
women are predominantly the offenders or victims. Prostitution, rape, and assault are cases in point. Much of the recent
literature attempts to place these offences in the general
context of heterosexual relations, in which, it is argued,
women are vulnerable to exploitation either commercially, as
in the case of prostitution, or physically and morally, as in the
case of rape and assault. On prostitution, see:

## 42 Work on Women

BARNETT, H. The Political Economy of Rape and Prostitition (*Review of Radical Political Economics* **8** (1) Spring 1976).

BRYAN, J. Apprenticeships in Prostitution (*Social Problems* **12** (3) Winter 1965).

— Occupational Ideologies of Call Girls, in E. Rubington and M. Weinberg (eds.), *Deviance: the Interactionist Perspective* (Macmillan, London, 1973).

BULLOUGH, V.L. *The History of Prostitution* (University Books, New York, 1964).

DAVIS, K. Prostitution, in R.K. Merton and R. Nisbet (eds.), *Contemporary Social Problems* (Harcourt Brace Jovanovich, New York, 1971).

GLOVER, E. *The Psychopathology of Prostitution* (ISTD Publication, London, 1969).

GREENWALD, H. *The Call Girl* (Ballantine, New York, 1958).

— *The Elegant Prostitute* (Walker and Co., New York, 1970).

HENRIQUES, F. *Prostitution and Society*, Vol. 3 of *Modern Sexuality* (MacGibbon and Kee, London, 1968).

MILLETT, K. *The Prostitution Papers* (Basic Books, New York, 1971 and Paladin, London, 1975).

WINN, D. *Prostitutes* (Hutchinson, London, 1974).

Whilst many feminist writers are ambivalent about the ethics of prostitution (see Kate Millett's 'Introduction' to *The Prostitution Papers*), the literature on rape and assault is far less equivocal. As Susan Brownmiller says, rape and the threat of rape '. . . is nothing more or less than a conscious process of intimidation by which *all* men keep *all* women in a state of fear' (*Against Our Will*). In short, rape is widely interpreted as a mechanism of social control. Other studies (such as Amir's) have examined the circumstances of rape and have shown, for example, that it is seldom unplanned and spontaneous, and the victim is often known:

AMIR, M. *Patterns in Forcible Rape* (The University of Chicago Press, Chicago, 1971).

BROWNMILLER, S. *Against Our Will* (Secker and Warburg, London, 1975).

BURGERS, A.W. and HOLSTROM, L. *Rape: Victims of Crisis* (R.J. Brady, Maryland, 1974).

GRIFFIN, S. Rape: The All American Crime (*Ramparts* **10** (3) September 1971).

JACKSON, S. The Social Context of Rape: Sexual Scripts and Motivation (*Women's Studies* **I** (1) 1978).

MEDEA, A. and THOMPSON, K. *Against Rape* (Farrar, Strauss and Ginous, New York, 1974).

REYNOLDS, J.M. Rape as Social Control (*Catalyst*, No. 8, Winter 1974).

RUSSELL, D. *The Politics of Rape: The Victim's Perspective* (Stein and Day, New York, 1975).

TONER, B. *The Facts of Rape* (Arrow Books, London, 1977).

WEIS, K. and BORGES, S. Victimology and Rape: The Case of the Legitimate Victim (*Issues in Criminology* **8** (2) 1973).

Research on assault, and particularly domestic violence, is expanding rapidly. A useful bibliography of American research entitled *A Comprehensive Bibliography: Domestic Violence, Crisis Intervention*, has recently been compiled by the Centre for Women Policy Studies and is available from C.W.P.S. at 2000, P Street N.W. , Suite 508, Washington D.C. 20036. The following studies deal primarily with violence in the home and the experience of battered wives:

FAULK, M. Men Who Assault Their Wives (*Medicine, Science and the Law* **14** (3) 1974).

GAYFORD, J. Battered Wives (*Medicine, Science and the Law* **15** (4) 1975).

GELLES, R. Abused Wives: Why Do They Stay? Available from the author at the Department of Sociology, University of New Hampshire, Durham, New Hampshire, 03824, USA.

## 44 Work on Women

— *The Violent Home: A Study of Physical Aggression between Husbands and Wives* (Sage, London, 1972).

GOODE, W. Force and Violence in the Family (*Journal of Marriage and the Family* **33** (4) November 1971).

H.M. GOVERNMENT *Report from the Select Committee on Violence in Marriage* (HMSO, London, 1975).

NSPCC *Yo Yo Children: A Study of Twenty Three Violent Matrimonial Cases* (National Society for the Prevention of Cruelty to Children, London, 1974).

PAHL, J. *A Refuge for Battered Women* (HMSO, London, 1978).

PIZZEY, E. *Scream Quietly or the Neighbours will hear* (Penguin, Harmondsworth, 1974).

STRAUS, M. *Sexuality Inequality, Cultural Norms and Wife Beating*. Available from the author at the Family Violence Research Program, University of New Hampshire, Durham, New Hampshire, 03824, USA.

WEIR, A. Battered Women, in, M. May (ed.) *Women in the Community* (Routledge and Kegan Paul, London, 1976).

# Literature, art,
# and popular culture

All literary and artistic works draw upon social life and thus reflect the stereotypes and values which mediate our perception of everyday life. This is particularly true of the mass media which typically presents romanticized and trivialized images of women as consumers, mothers, sexual partners, and wives. The production and ideological significance of this process is analysed and discussed in the following:

COURTNEY, A. and LOCKERETZ, S.W. A Woman's Place: An Analysis of the Roles Portrayed by Women in Magazine Advertisements (*Journal of Marketing Research*, February 8, 1971).

FLORA, C.B. The Passive Female: Her Comparative Image by Class and Culture in Women's Magazine Fiction (*Journal of Marriage and the Family* **33** August 1971).

FRIEDMAN, L. *Sex Role Stereotyping in the Mass Media* (Garland, New York, 1977).

HASKELL, M. *From Reverence to Rape: The Treatment of Women in Movies* (Holt Rinehart and Winston, New York, 1974).

JOHNSTONE, C. (ed.) *Notes on Women's Cinema* (Society for Education in Film and Cinema, London, 1973).

KING, J. and STOTT. M. (eds.) *Is This Your Life? Images of Women in the Media* (Virago, London, 1977).

MELLEN, J. *Women and their Sexuality in the New Film* (Dell, New York, 1973).

MILLUM, T. *Images of Women: Advertising in Woman's Magazines* (Rowman and Littlefield, New York, 1975).

TUCHMAN, G., DANIELS, A.K. and BENET, J. *Hearth and Home: Images of Women in the Mass Media* (Oxford University Press, New York, 1978).

WHITE, C. *Women's Magazines: A Sociological Inquiry* (Michael Joseph, London, 1970).

WINSHIP, J. A Woman's World: Woman: An Ideology of Femininity, in, Women's Studies Group, Centre for Contemporary Cultural Studies, The University of Birmingham, *Women Take Issue*, (Hutchinson, London, 1978).

Similarly, others have examined the images of women in literature and popular fiction:

AUERBACH, N. *Communities of Women: An Idea in Fiction* (Harvard University Press, Cambridge, Mass., 1978).

BASCH, F. *Relative Creatures: Victorian Women in Society and the Novel, 1837–1876* (Allen Lane, London, 1974).

BAYM, N. *Women's Fiction: A Guide to Novels by and about Women in America, 1820–1870* (Cornell University Press, Ithaca, N.Y., 1978).

BERNIKOW, L. (ed.) *The World Split Open: Four Centuries of Women Poets in England and America, 1552–1950* (Vintage Books, New York, 1974).

CALDER, J. *Women and Marriage in Victorian Fiction* (Oxford University Press, Oxford, 1976).

ELLMANN, M. *Thinking about Women* (Virago, London, 1979).

EWBANK, I.S. *Their Proper Sphere* (Harvard University Press, Cambridge, Mass., 1966).

GOODE, J. Women and the Literary Text, in A. Oakley and J. Mitchell (eds.), *The Rights and Wrongs of Women* (Penguin, Harmondsworth, 1976).

GOULIANOS, J. (ed.) *By a Woman Writt: Literature from Six Centuries by and about Women* (Penguin, Baltimore, 1973).

HARDWICK, E. *Seduction and Betrayal: Women and Literature* (Random House, New York, 1974).

KAPLAN, S.J. *Feminine Consciousness in the Modern British Novel* (Illinois University Press, Urbana, 1975).

MARDER, H. *Feminism and Art: A Study of Virginia Woolf* (Chicago University Press, Chicago, 1975).

MARKS, E. Women and Literature in France (*Signs* **3** (4) 1978).

MILLETT, K. *Sexual Politics* (Doubleday, New York, 1970).

NIGHTINGALE, C. Sex Roles in Children's Literature (*The Assistant Librarian* October 1972).

NILSEN, A.P. Women in Children's Literature (*College English* **32** May 1971).

ROBERTS, H. Propaganda and Ideology in Women's Fiction, in D. Laurenson (ed.), *The Sociology of Literature: Applied Studies* (University of Keele, *Sociological Review Monograph* No. 26, 1978).

SHOWALTER, E. *A Literature of their Own* (Princeton University Press, Princeton, 1976).

SPACKS, P.M. *The Female Imagination* (Knopf, New York, 1975).

TRILLING, D. The Image of Women in Contemporary Literature, in R.J. Lifton (ed.), *The Woman in America* (The Beacon Press, Boston, 1964).

WATSON, B.B. On Power and the Literary Text (*Signs* **1** (1) Autumn 1975).

In addition, a few writers have explored the symbolic significance attributed to women in language, religion, myth, and sexual humour :

BACHOFEN, J. *Myth, Religion and Mother Right* (Bollingen, Princeton, 1967).

BULLOUGH, V.L. *The Subordinate Sex: A History of Attitudes*

48 Work on Women

*toward Women* (Penguin, Harmondsworth and Baltimore, 1973).

ELIADE, M. *Gods, Goddesses and Myths of Creation* (Harper and Row, New York, 1974).

FARRER, C.R. *Women and Folklore* (University of Texas Press, Austin, Texas, 1976).

HAYS, H. *The Dangerous Sex: The Myth of Feminine Evil* (Pocket Books, New York, 1966).

LAKOFF, R. *Language and Woman's Place* (Harper and Row, New York, 1975).

LEGMAN, C. *The Rationale of the Dirty Joke: An Analysis of Sexual Humour* (Jonathan Cape, London, 1972).

LIPMAN-BLUMEN, J. How Ideology shapes Women's Lives (*Scientific American*, No. 226, January 1972).

RUETHER, R. (ed.) *Religion and Sexism: Images of Woman in the Jewish and Christian Traditions* (Simon and Schuster, New York, 1974).

TAVARD, G. *Woman in Christian Tradition* (University of Indiana Press, Notre Dame, 1973).

THORNE, B., and HENLEY, N. (eds.) *Language and Sex: Difference and Dominance* (Newbury House Publishers, Rowley, Mass., 1975).

WARNER, M. *Alone of all her Sex : The Myth and the Cult of the Virgin Mary* (Knopf, London and New York, 1976).

The comparatively minor contribution of women to artistic and cultural life has remained a problem since it was raised by Virginia Woolf in her classic essay *A Room of One's Own*. The reasons for the small number of women artists, writers and intellectuals are further explored in the following:

ELBERT, S. and GLASTONBURY, M. *Inspiration and Drudgery: Notes on Literature and Domestic Labour in the Nineteenth Century* (Women's Research and Resources Centre, Explorations in Feminism, No. 5, London, 1978).

HESS, T. and BAKER, E. (eds.) *Art and Sexual Politics* (Macmillan, New York and London, 1971).

MOERS, E. *Literary Women* (Doubleday, New York, 1976).

NOCHLIN, L. Why have there been no great Women Artists? (*Arts News*, January 1971).

OLSEN, T. When Women Don't Write, in S. Koppelman (ed.), *Images of Women in Fiction: Feminist Perspectives* (Cornillon, Ohio, 1973).

PETERSEN, K. and WILSON, J. *Women Artists: Recognition and Reappraisal from the Early Middle Ages to the Twentieth Century* (Harper and Row, New York, 1976).

TUCHMAN, G. Women and the Creation of Culture (*Sociological Inquiry*, February 1975).

WOOLF, V. *A Room of One's Own* (Hogarth Press 1928; republished Penguin, 1963).

# Cross-cultural studies

On a global scale, relations between the sexes vary greatly: in some societies women exercise considerable influence and social power. However, there are few, if any, societies in which women surpass the power and authority of men. Cross-cultural studies widely confirm this view. Reviewing the evidence, Rosaldo (1974) remarks, '. . . women may be important, powerful and influential, but it seems that, relative to men of their age and social status, women everywhere lack generally recognised and culturally valued authority' (*Woman, Culture and Society*). Furthermore, Evans-Pritchard suggests, '. . . regardless of the form of social structure, men are always in the ascendency, and this is perhaps the more evident the higher the civilisation' (*The Position of Women in Primitive Societies and our Own*). The question raised by these observations – which are widely reported elsewhere – is why is this so? Feminist anthropologists have suggested two kinds of answer: some have denied that male domination is a truly universal fact and refer to specific ethnographic studies – such as Rattray on the Ashanti – to support their case; others (e.g. Fee, Ardener, and Slocum) have argued that since anthropologists are generally men (or at least, as Ardener suggests, trained to think like men) they have interpreted other cultures from a male point of view, drawing ethnographic data largely from male informants and imposing upon all societies the hierarchical assumptions of their own North American and European cultures. However, even if these exceptions and qualifications are allowed, the problem remains of why, in most if not all of the societies studied, women are perceived as culturally inferior to men. The theoretical implications of this problem are considered in the following:

ARDENER, E. Belief and the Problem of Women, in Jean La Fontaine (ed.), *The Interpretation of Ritual* (Tavistock, London, 1972).

For a comment on the above essay by the same author see:
— Belief and the Problem of Women, in S. Ardener (ed.), *Perceiving Women* (Malaby Press, London, 1975).

BROWN, J.K. A Note on the Division of Labour by Sex (*American Anthropologist* **72** 1970).

CRITIQUE OF ANTHROPOLOGY *Women's Issue* No 9/10, 1977 (available from Critique of Anthropology, PO Box 178, London WCIE 6BU).

DOUGLAS, M. *Purity and Danger* (Routledge and Kegan Paul, London, 1966).

ENGELS, F. *The Origin of the Family, Private Property and the State* (Progress Publishers, Moscow, 1964).

E. EVANS-PRITCHARD *The Position of Women in Primitive Societies and our Own* (Bedford College, London, 1955).

FEE, E. The Sexual Politics of Victorian Social Anthropology (*Feminist Studies*, **1** (23) 1973).

FRIEDL, E. The Position of Women: Appearance and Reality (*Anthropological Quarterly* **40** (3) 1967).

— *Women and Men: An Anthropologist's View* (Holt, Rinehart and Winston, New York, 1975).

GIELE, J.Z. Centuries of Womanhood: An Evolutionary Perspective on the Feminine Role (*Women's Studies* **1** 1972).

JACOBS, S. *Women in Perspective: A Guide for Cross Cultural Studies* (University of Illinois Press, Urbana, 1974).

## 52 Work on Women

MEAD, M. *Male and Female* (William Morris, New York, 1949).

MURDOCK, G.P. Comparative Data on the Division of Labour by Sex (*Social Forces* **15** 1937).

ORTNER, S. Is Female to Male as Nature is to Culture? (*Feminist Studies* **1** (5) 1972).

RATTRAY, R. *Ashanti* (Clarendon, Oxford, 1969, first published in 1923).

REITER, R. (ed.) *Towards an Anthropology of Women* (The Monthly Review Press, New York and London, 1975).

ROGERS, S. Woman's Place: A Critical Review of Anthropological Theory (*Comparative Studies in Society and History* **20** (1) January 1978).

ROSALDO, M. and LAMPHERE, L. (eds.) *Woman, Culture and Society* (Stanford University Press, Stanford, 1974).

SAFILIOS-ROTHSCHILD, C. A Cross Cultural Examination of Women's Familial, Educational and Occupational Options (*Acta Sociologica*, **14** (1/2) Spring 1971).

SCHLEGEL, A. (ed.) *Sexual Stratification: A Cross Cultural View* (Columbia University Press, New York, 1977).

SLOCUM, S. Woman the Gatherer: The Male Bias in Anthropology, in R. Reiter (ed.), *Towards an Anthropology of Women* (Monthly Review Press, New York and London, 1975).

Whatever their symbolic status, women frequently play a crucial role in economic development and social change. As the studies by Boserup and Mintz suggest, women are often key agents in the control and distribution of resources through inheritance, marriage, and trade. Furthermore, in spite of socially inferior positions, women often have a great deal of autonomy in manipulating important areas of social and political life (see, in particular, Caplan and Maher below).

ALLEN, J.V. Sitting on a Man: Colonialism and the Lost

Institutions of Igbo Women (*Canadian Journal of African Studies* **6** (165) 1972).

ANTHROPOLOGICAL QUARTERLY *Appearance and Reality: The Position of Women in Mediterranean Societies* **40** (3) 1967.

APPADORAI. A. (ed.) *The Status of Women in South Asia* (Orient Longmans, Bombay 1954).

BOSERUP, E. *Women's Role in Economic Development* (St Martin's Press, New York, 1970).

BROWN, P. and BUCHBINDER, G. (eds.) *Man and Woman in the New Guinea Highlands* (American Anthropological Association, Washington, D.C., 1976).

CAPLAN, P. and BUJRA, J. (eds.) *Women United, Women Divided* (Tavistock, London, 1978; University of Indiana Press, Bloomington, 1979).

DAHLSTROM, E. (ed.) *The Changing Roles of Men and Women* (Beacon, Boston, 1967).

DEERE, C.D. Rural Women's Subsistence Production in the Capitalist Periphery (*Review of Radical Political Economics* **8** (1) Spring 1976).

— Changing Social Relations of Production and Peruvian Peasant Women's Work (*Latin American Perspectives* **IV** (1 & 2) 1977).

DRAPER, P. Kung Women: Contrasts in Sexual Egalitarianism in Foraging and Sedentary Contexts, in R. Reiter (ed.), *Towards an Anthropology of Women*.

GIELE, J. and SMOCK, A.C. (eds.) *Women: Role and Status in Eight Countries* (Wiley, New York, 1977).

HANMER, J. Clitoridectomy and Infibulation: The Sexual Mutilation of Women (Women's Research and Resources Centre, London, 1977).

KABERRY, P. *Aboriginal Woman: Sacred and Profane* (Routledge, London, 1939).

— *Women of the Grassfields: A Study of the Economic Position of Women in Bamenda.* (Gregg Press, Farnborough, 1968).

LEAVITH, R. (ed.) *Women Cross Culturally: Change and Challenge* (Mouton, The Hague, 1975).

LEITH-ROSS, S. *African Women: A Study of the Ibo of Nigeria* (Faber and Faber, London, 1939).

LEVINE, R. Sex Roles and Economic Change in Africa (*Ethnology* 1966).

LINTON, R. Women in the Family, in M. Sussman (ed.), *A Source Book in Marriage and the Family* (Houghton Mifflin, Boston, 1962).

MAHER, V. Kin, Clients and Accomplices: Relationships among Women in Morocco, in D. Barker and S. Allen (eds.) *Sexual Divisions and Society: Process and Change* (Tavistock, London, 1976).

MATTHIASSON, C.J. (ed.) *Many Sisters: Women in Cross Cultural Perspective* (The Free Press, New York, 1974).

MCCALL, R. Trade and the Role of the Wife in a Modern West African Town, in A. Southall (ed.), *Social Change in Modern Africa* (Oxford University Press, London, 1963).

MERNISSI, F. *Beyond the Veil: Male/Female Dynamics in a Modern Muslim Society* (John Wiley, New York, 1975).

MINTZ, S. Men, Women and Trade (*Comparative Studies in Society and History* **13** 1971).

MOREWEDGE, R.T. (ed.) *The Role of Women in the Middle Ages* (State University of New York Press, Albany, 1975).

MURPHY, Y. and R. *Women of the Forest* (Columbia University Press, New York, 1974).

POMEROY, S. *Goddesses, Whores, Wives and Slaves: Women in Classical Antiquity* (Schocken, New York, 1975).

PORTER, M. and VENNING, C. *Church, Law and Society* (University of Michigan, Women's Studies Papers **1** (2) 1974).

ROGERS, S. Female Forms of Power and the Myth of Male Dominance: A Model of Male/Female Interaction in Peasant Society (*American Ethnologist* **2** 1975).

ROSENBLATT, P., and CUNNINGHAM, M. Sex Differences in Cross Cultural Perspective, in B. Lloyd and J. Archer (eds.), *Exploring Sex Differences* (Academic Press, New York, 1976).

SIGNS *Women and National Development* (Special Issue, **3** (1) Autumn, 1977).

STRATHERN, M. *Women in Between: Female Roles in a Male World: Mount Hagen, New Guinea* (Seminar Press, London, 1972).

STUARD, S. (ed.) *Women in Mediaval Society* (University of Pennsylvania Press, Philadelphia, 1976).

SULLEROT, E. *Woman, Society and Change* (World University Library, London, 1971).

THOMPSON, R. *Women in Stuart England and America* (Routledge and Kegan Paul, London, 1974).

TIGER, L. and SHEPHER, J. *Women in the Kibbutz* (Harcourt, Brace, Jovanovich, New York, 1975).

WARD, B. (ed.) *Women in the New Asia* (UNESCO, Paris, 1963).

WIPPER, A. The Roles of African Women: Past, Present and Future *(Canadian Journal of African Studies* No. 6, 1972).

YOUSSEF, N. *Women and Work in Developing Societies* (University of California Press, Berkeley, 1974).

ZAIDI, S. Changing Role and Status of Professional Women in Pakistan *(Pakistan Journal of Psychology* **4** (1–2) June 1971).

Finally, the following items deal with the position of women in socialist societies. Although many feminists believe socialism will radically transform the status of women, evidence from China, Eastern Europe, and the Soviet Union suggests the socialization of production has so far done little to alter the traditional division of labour, or allowed women a significantly more equal role in social and political life. See:

## 56 Work on Women

ALLENDORF, M. *Women in Socialist Society* (International Publishers, New York, 1975).

BOXER, M. and QUATAERT, J. (eds.) *Socialist Women* (Elsevier Publishing Company, The Hague, 1978).

BROWN, D. (ed.) *The Role and Status of Women in the Soviet Union* (Teachers College Press, New York, 1968).

CROLL, E. *Feminism and Socialism in China* (Routledge and Kegan Paul, London and Boston, 1979).

DAVIN, D. Women in Revolutionary China, in A. Oakley and J. Mitchell (eds.), *The Rights and Wrongs of Women* (Penguin, Harmondsworth, 1976).

— *Woman Work: Women and the Party in Revolutionary China* (Oxford University Press, New York, 1976).

DODGE, N. *Women in the Soviet Economy* (Johns Hopkins Press, Baltimore, 1966).

LOBODZINSKA, B. The Education and Employment of Women in Contemporary Poland (*Signs* **3** (3) Spring 1978).

MANDEL, W. *Soviet Women* (Anchor Books, New York, 1975).

PRUITT, I. *The Daughter of Han: An Autobiography of a Chinese Working Woman* (Stanford University Press, Stanford, 1968).

ROWBOTHAM, S. *Women, Resistance and Revolution* (Allen Lane, London, 1972).

SALAFF, J. and MERKLE, J. Women in Revolution: The Lesson of the Soviet Union and China (*Socialist Revolution* July/August 1970).

SCOTT, H. *Does Socialism Liberate Women? Experiences from Eastern Europe* (The Beacon Press, Boston, 1974).

SNOW, H. *Women in Modern China* (Mouton, The Hague, 1967).

WEINBAUM, B. Women in the Transition to Socialism: Perspectives on the Chinese Case (*Review of Radical Political Economics* **8** (1) Spring 1976).

WOLF, M. *Women in Chinese Society* (Stanford University Press, Stanford, 1975).

YOUNG, M. (ed.) *Women in China: Studies in Social Change and Feminism* (Centre for Chinese Studies, University of Michigan, Ann Arbor, 1973).

# Social psychological
# perspectives

The evidence of cross-cultural studies has persuaded many anthropologists that the secondary status of women is a truly universal social fact. However, whether the subordinate position of women is due to innate differences between the sexes or purely social causes is inevitably complicated by the fact that in all societies sexual differences are socially elaborated and distorted by different patterns of socialization and role allocation. As in all 'nature-nurture' debates, the problem is one of disentangling natural attributes from cultural traits. This is especially difficult when the attributes in question are believed to be inherently psychological. Thus, while many psychologists have argued that women are more passive, subjective, and nurturant, but less aggressive, independent and intellectually less versatile than men, (see, for example, Corinne Hutt, *Males and Females*), others have questioned the idea of a distinctively 'female personality' on the grounds that there are few, if any, significant differences between women and men that cannot be explained in specifically social terms (see Maccoby 1966). The existing literature on the subject is extensive, but inconclusive. The following consider the evidence from various points of view:

BARDWICK, J.N. (ed.) *Readings on the Psychology of Women* (Harper and Row, New York, 1972).

BARDWICK, J. *Psychology of Women: A Study of Biocultural Conflicts* (Harper and Row, New York, 1971).

BIERI, J., BRADBURN, W., and GALINSKY, D. Sex Differences in Perceptual Behaviour (*Journal of Personality* **26** (1) 1958).

CARLSON, R. Understanding Women: Implications for Personality Theory and Research (*Journal of Social Issues* **18** (2) 1972).

COWARD, R. and ELLIS, J. *Language and Materialism* (Routledge and Kegan Paul, London, 1977).

DEUTSCH, H. *The Psychology of Women* (Grune and Stratton, New York, 1944).

FREUD, S. *Three Essays on the Theory of Sexuality* (Hogarth Press, London, 1970). This also contains an extremely useful bibliography of Freud's work)

FREUD, S. Some Psychological Consequences of the Anatomical Distinction between the Sexes, in D. Schaeffer (ed.), *Sex Differences in Personality* (Brooks Cole, California, 1971).

FREUD, S. The Psychology of Women, in, *New Introductory Lectures* (W.W. Norton, New York, 1933).

FRIEDMAN, R.C. *Sex Differences in Behaviour* (Wiley, New York, 1974).

GARAI, J. and SCHEINFIELD, A. *Sex Differences in Mental and Behavioural Traits* (Genetic Psychology Monographs, No. 77, 1968).

HORNEY, K. *Feminine Psychology* (Norton, New York, 1967).

HUTT, C. *Males and Females* (Penguin, Harmondsworth, 1972).

KAPLAN, A.G. and BEAN, J.P. *Beyond Sex Role Stereotypes* (Little Brown, Boston, 1976).

LLOYD, B. and ARCHER, J. (eds.) *Exploring Sex Differences* (Academic Press, New York, 1976).

MACCOBY, E. (ed.) *The Development of Sex Differences* (Stanford University Press, Stanford, 1966).

MACCOBY, E. and JACKLIN, C. *The Psychology of Sex Differences* (Stanford University Press, Stanford, 1974).

MITCHELL, J. *Psychoanalysis and Feminism* (Allen Lane, London, 1974).

MONEY, J. and EHRHARDT, A. *Man and Woman, Boy and Girl: The Differentiation and Dimorphism of Gender from Conception to Maturity* (Johns Hopkins University Press, Baltimore, 1972).

SCHAEFFER, D. (ed.) *Sex Differences in Personality* (Brooke Cole, California, 1971).

SHERMAN, J. *On the Psychology of Women* (Charles Thomas, Springfield, 1971).

STOLLER, R.J. The Sense of Femaleness (*Psychoanalytic Quarterly* **37** 1968).

Even if there were conclusive evidence of invariant and distinctly feminine psychological traits, it would not necessarily follow that these characteristics are instinctive or innate. Different patterns of sexual socialization develop different abilities, responses, and traits and similarly suppress others socially expected of the opposite sex. As Bailyn, Komarovsky, and others point out, the socialization of women in industrial societies tends to suppress abilities and talents valued in men. Moreover, the incompatibility of traditional notions of femininity with intellectual competence and worldly success often results in what Horner describes as a 'fear of success'. These and other psychological consequences of sexual socialization are discussed in the following:

BAILYN, L. Notes on the Role of Choice in the Psychology of Professional Women, in R.J. Lifton (ed.), *The Woman in America* (The Beacon Press, Boston, 1964).

BARRY, H., BACON, M. and CHILD, I. A Cross Cultural Survey of Some Sex Differences in Socialisation (*Journal of Abnormal Psychology* **55** 1957).

BROVERMAN, I.K., BROVERMAN, D., CLARKSON, F., ROSENKRANTZ, P., VOGEL, S. Sex Role Stereotypes: A

Current Appraisal (*Journal of Social Issues* **28** (2) 1972).

FARBER, S. and WILSON, R. (eds.) *The Potential of Women* (McGraw Hill, New York, 1963).

FROSCHL, M. It's never too early: Sex Role Stereotyping in the Pre-School Years (*Colloquoy* **6** (9) November 1973).

HOFFMAN, L.W. Early Childhood Experiences and Women's Achievement Motives (*Journal of Social Issues* **28** (2) 1972).

HORNER, M. A Bright Woman is Caught in a Double Bind (*Psychology Today* **3** (6) November 1969).

— Femininity and Successful Achievement: A Basic Inconsistency, in J. Bardwick, E. Douvan, M. Horner and D. Gutman (eds.), *Feminine Personality and Conflict* (Brooks Cole, California, 1970).

— Fail, Bright Women, in A. Theodore (ed.), *The Professional Woman* (Schenkman, Cambridge, Mass., 1971).

— Toward an Understanding of Achievement Related Conflicts in Women (*Journal of Social Issues* **28** (2) 1972).

KLEIN, V. *The Feminine Character: History of an Ideology* (Routledge and Kegan Paul, London, 1946).

KOMAROVSKY, M. Cultural Contradictions and Sex Roles (*American Journal of Sociology* **52** November, 1946).

— *Women in the Modern World: Their Education and Their Dilemmas* (Houghton Mifflin, Boston, 1953).

LEVY, B. Sex Role Socialisation in Schools, in *Sex Role Stereotyping in the Schools* (National Education Association, Washington, 1973).

McROBBIE, A. Working Class Girls and the Culture of Femininity, in, the Women's Studies Group, Centre for Contemporary Cultural Studies, *Women Take Issue* (Hutchinson, London, 1978).

PARSONS, J.E. Cognitive Developmental Factors in Emerging Sex Differences in Achievement Related Expectations (*Journal of Social Issues* **32** 1976).

OLESON, V. Militants in a Woman's Profession: Psychological Characteristics of Partisans and Critics of a Nurses'

Strike (*Psychological Reports* **32** 1973).

RAPOPORT, R. and R. Early and Later Experiences as Determinants of Adult Behaviour (*British Journal of Sociology* **22** March, 1971).

SHAINESS, N. Images of Women Present and Past: Overt and Obscured, (*American Journal of Psychotherapy* **13** 1969).

SOLOMON, B. Historical Determinants and Successful Professional Women, in R.B. Kundsin (ed.), *Women and Success: The Anatomy of Achievement* (Morrow, New York, 1974).

STEINMANN, A., LEVI, J. and FOX, D. Self Concept of College Women compared with their Concept of Ideal Woman and Men's Ideal Women (*Journal of Counselling Psychology* **11** (4) 1964).

SUTHERLAND, S. The Unambitious Female: Women's Low Professional Aspirations (*Signs* **3** (4) Summer 1978).

TRESEMER, D. Do Women Fear Success? (*Signs* **1** (4) Summer 1976).

WEITZMAN, L. and EIFLER, D. Sex Role Socialisation in Picture Books for Pre-School Children (*American Journal of Sociology* **77** (6) May 1972).

The pressures on women to conform to a narrow set of sexual and maternal expectations are illustrated and discussed in the following:

BARKER-BENFIELD, B. The Spermatic Economy: A Nineteenth Century View of Sexuality (*Feminist Studies* **1** 1972).

BREEN, D. *The Birth of a First Child: Towards an Understanding of Femininity* (Tavistock, London, 1975).

BURNISTON, S., MORT, F. and WEEDON, C. Psychoanalysis and the Cultural Acquisition of Sexuality and Subjectivity, in, Women's Studies Group, Centre for Contemporary Cultural Studies, University of Birmingham, *Women Take Issue* (Hutchinson, London, 1978).

DEGLER, C. What ought to be and what was: women's sexuality in the nineteenth century (*American Historical Review* **79** 1974).

HITE, S. *The Hite Report: A Nationwide Study of Female Sexuality* (Macmillan, New York, 1976; Talmy Franklin, London, 1977).

HOFFMAN, M. Assumptions in Sex Education Books (*Educational Review* **27** (3) 1975).

HOLLINGSWORTH, L. Social Devices for Impelling Women to Bear and Rear Children (*American Journal of Sociology* **22** July, 1916).

HORNEY, K. The Flight from Womanhood: The Masculinity Complex in Women, as viewed by Men and Women (*International Journal of Psychoanalysis* **7** 1926).

JACKSON, S. *On the Social Construction of Female Sexuality* (Women's Research and Resources Centre, Explorations in Feminism, London, 1978).

KINSEY, A.C., POMEROY, W.B., MARTIN, C.E., GEVHARDT, P.H. Sexual Behaviour in the Human Female (W.B. Saunders, Philadelphia, 1953).

KOEDT, A. The Myth of the Vaginal Orgasm, in L. Tanner (ed.), *Voices from Women's Liberation*, (New American Library, New York, 1971).

MACINTYRE, S. Who Wants Babies? The Social Construction of Instincts, in D. Barker and S. Allen (eds.), *Sexual Divisions and Society, Process and Change* (Tavistock, London, 1976).

— *Single and Pregnant* (Croom Helm, London, 1977).

MASTERS, W. and JOHNSON, V. *Human Sexual Response* (Little Brown, Boston, 1966).

NEWTON, N. *Maternal Emotions* (P.B. Hoeber, New York, 1955).

RICH, A. *Of Woman Born: Motherhood as Experience and Institution* (Norton, New York, 1976 and Virago, London, 1977).

SAGHIR, M. and ROBINS, E. *Male and Female Homosexuality*

(Williams and Wilkins Co., Baltimore, 1973).

VINCENT, C. *Unmarried Mothers* (Free Press, New York, 1961).

WEISSTEIN, N. Kinde, Kuche, Kirche: Psychology Constructs the Female, in V. Gornick and B. Moran (eds.), *Women in Sexist Society* (Basic Books, New York, 1971).

WHITING, P. Female Sexuality: Its Political Implications, in M. Wandor (ed.), *The Body Politic* (Stage One Publications, London, 1972).

The tendency for medical practitioners to perceive deviations from cultural norms of femininity as symptoms of inadequate personality or psychoneurotic complaints, is well documented by the American Psychological Association and by Broverman, Lennane, and others below. While this tendency undoubtedly contributes to the high rates of treated neuroses amongst women, others have suggested that the increasing prevalence of psychiatric disturbance, especially amongst married women, could be associated with changing role expectations which compound the anxieties and uncertainties in a woman's life (see Gove and Tudor). It is evident, however, that not all women are equally at risk: Brown and Harris report that the likelihood of depression amongst women who share intimate friendships, or who go out to work, is significantly less than amongst those who are personally isolated or who remain at home with young children all day. For a detailed discussion of these and other factors affecting women's vulnerability to psychiatric disorder, see Brown and Harris' excellent study, *Social Origins of Depression*, and also Grunebaum, below:

AMERICAN PSYCHOLOGICAL ASSOCIATION Sex Bias and Sex Role Stereotyping in Psychotherapeutic Practice: Report (*American Psychologist* **30** 1975).

BAKER MILLER, J. *Psychoanalysis and Women* (Penguin, Harmondsworth, 1973).

BARRET, C., BERG, P. EATON, E. and POMEROY, L. Implications of Women's Liberation and the Future of Psychotherapy (*Psychotherapy: Theory, Research and Practice* **11** 1974).

BART, P. Mother Portnoy's Complaint (*Transaction* **8** Nov–Dec 1970).

— The Myth of a Value Free Psychotherapy, in W. Bell and J. Man (eds.), *Sociology and the Future* (The Russell Sage Foundation, New York, 1971).

BROVERMAN, I.K. *et. al.* Sex Role Stereotypes and Clinical Judgements of Mental Health (*Journal of Consulting Psychology* **34** 1970).

BROWN, G. and HARRIS, T. *The Social Origins of Depression: A Study of Psychiatric Disorder in Women* (Tavistock, London, 1978; Free Press, New York, 1979).

CHESLER, P. *Women and Madness* (Doubleday, Garden City, N.Y., 1972).

COWARD, R., LIPSHITZ, S. and COWIE, E. Psychoanalysis and Patriarchal Structures, in *Papers on Patriarchy* (Women's Publishing Collective, Lewes, 1976).

GOVE, W. The Relationship between Sex Roles, Marital Status and Mental Illness (*Social Forces* **51** 1972).

GOVE, W. and TUDOR, J. Adult Sex Roles and Mental Illness (*American Journal of Sociology* **78** 1972).

GRUNEBAUM, H., WEISS, J., COHLER, B., HARTMAN, C. and GALLANT D. *Mentally Ill Mothers and their Children* (Chicago University Press, Chicago, 1975).

LENNANE, A.K. and LENNANE, R.J. Alleged Psychogenic Disorders in Women: A Possible Manifestation of Sexual Prejudice (*New England Journal of Medicine* **228** (6) 1973).

MOULTON, R. Some Effects of the New Feminism (*American Journal of Psychiatry* **134** (1) January 1977).

# Additional bibliographies, general reviews of literature, feminist journals and periodicals

ADDITIONAL BIBLIOGRAPHIES

AL-QAZZAZ, Ayad, *Women in the Middle East and North Africa : An Annotated Bibliography* (Centre for Middle Eastern Studies, University of Texas, Middle East Monographs, No. 2, Austin, 1977).

ARORA, Ved, *Women: A Selected Bibliography* (Regina Public Library, Saskatchewan, 1972).

ASTIN, H., SUNIEWICK, N., DWEK, S., *Women: A Bibliography on their Education and Careers* (Human Service Press, Washington, D.C., 1971).

BAER, H. and SHERIF, C., (eds.), *A Topical Bibliography on the Psychology of Women* (American Psychological Association, 1200, 17th Street N.W., Washington, 20036, 1974).

BARKER, D.L. and ALLEN, S. Bibliography, pp 246-260, in *Dependence and Exploitation in Work and Marriage* (Longman, Harlow, 1976).

BARNARD COLLEGE, The Barnard College Women's Center, New York, 10027 has produced the following bibliographies:
— *Women's Work and Women's Studies 1971*, edited by K. Drake, D. Marks and M. Wexford.
— *Women's Work and Women's Studies 1972*, edited by D.

Ellis, K. Graves, K. Grimstead, D. Marks, F. Pollack, J. Thompson and and M. Wexford.

— *Women's Work and Women's Studies 1973–1974* edited by B. Friedman, G. Greenstein, E. Kofran, F. Pollack and J. Williamson.

A list of publications of the Center may be obtained from the Barnard College Women's Center, 100, Barnard Hall, Broadway and 117th Street, New York, 10027.

BUSINESS AND PROFESSIONAL WOMEN'S FOUNDATION, *Women Executives: A Selected Bibliography* (The Business and Professional Women's Foundation, Washington, 1970) and, *Women and Work in U.S. History: An Annotated Selected Bibliography.* (Both publications available from the Business and Professional Women's Foundation, 2012 Massachusetts Avenue, N.W., Washington, D.C. 20036, 1976).

BUVINIC, M., *Women and World Development : An Annotated Bibliography* (American Association for the Advancement of Science, for the Overseas Development Council, 1717, Massachusetts Avenue, Washington, D.C., 20036, 1976).

CAREY, E., *Women, Sexuality, Psychology and Psychotherapy: A Bibliography* (Womanspace, 636 Beacon Street, Boston, Mass., 1977).

CENTRE FOR WOMEN POLICY STUDIES, *Bibliography on Women Entrepreneurs* (Washington, D.C., The Centre for Women Policy Studies, 1974).

CHAFF, S. (ed.) *Women in Medicine: A Bibliography of the Literature on Women Physicians* (Scarecrow Press, Metuchen, N. Jersey, 1977).

CISLER, LUCINDA, *Women: A Bibliography* (editions published in 1968, 1969, 1970; available from Box 240, New York, N.Y. 10024).

CROMWELL, P.E., *Women and Mental Health : Selected, Annotated References 1970–1973* (The National Institute of Mental Health, Division of Scientific and Technical Information, Maryland, 20852, 1974).

CUSICK, J., *A Resource List for Non-Sexist Education* (The National Foundation for the Improvement of Education, Washington, D.C., 1976).

DANIELS, A.K., *A Survey of Research Concerns on Women's Issues* (The National Science Foundation, Washington, D.C., October 1973).

DAVIS, A., *A Bibliography on Women* (Science History Publications, New York, 1974).

DAVIS, L.G., *The Black Woman in American Society: A Selected Annotated Bibliography* (G.K. Hall, Boston, 1975).

DEGEN, M.H., *Women and Employment: An Annotated Bibliography* (The Business Division, The District of Columbia Public Library, Washington, D.C., 1974).

DOCUMENTATION FRANCAISE, *Les Femmes: Guide Bibliographique* (Documentation Française, Paris, 1974).

EICHLER, M., *An Annotated Selected Bibliography of Bibliographies on Women* (Association of Universities and Colleges of Canada, Ottawa, 1973).

FAULDER, C., JACKSON, C., LEWIS, M., *The Women's Directory* (Virago, London, 1976).

FREEMAN, L., *The Changing Role of Women: A Bibliography* (Sacramento State College Library, Sacramento, 1972).

HABER, BARBARA, *Women in America: A Guide to Books, 1963–1975* (G.K. Hall, Boston, 1978).

HER STORY, Microfilm collection of documents on women in history, produced by the Women's History Library, Berkeley, California and supplemented annually (from 1971) by the Women's History Research Centre, Berkeley, California.

INTERNATIONAL JOURNAL OF URBAN AND REGIONAL RESEARCH, Special Issue on *Women in the City*, Autumn 1978.

JACOBS, S.E., *Women in Perspective: A Guide for Cross Cultural Studies* (University of Illinois Press, Urbana, 1974).

JAVONVICH, JOANN, *Women and Psychology* (Goddard Graduate School for Social Change, Feminist Studies Programme. Available from 5, Upland Road, Cambridge, Mass. 02140).

JOYCE, LINDA, *An Annotated Bibliography of Women in Rural America* (Penn State University, Department of Agricultural Economics, 1976).

KING, Judith, *Women's Studies Sourcebook* (Grand Valley Colleges Library, Allendale, USA, 1976).

KNASTER, M., *Women in Spanish Amercia: An Annotated Bibliography from Pre-Conquest to Contemporary Times* (G.K. Hall, Boston, 1977).

KRICHMAR, A., *The Women's Rights Movement in the United States, 1848–1970: A Bibliography and Sourcebook* (The Scarecrow Press, Metuchen, New Jersey, 1972).

— *The Women's Movement in the Seventies: An International English Language Bibliography* (Scarecrow Press, Metuchen, New Jersey, 1977).

LEVITT, M., *Women's Role in American Politics: A Bibliography* (Council of Planning Libraries, Washington, D.C., 1973).

LYNN, N., *Research Guide in Women's Studies* (General Learning Press, Morristown, New Jersey, 1974).

MASSACHUSETTS INSTITUTE OF TECHNOLOGY, Human Studies Collection, Humanties Library, *Women's Studies Bibliography*, (M.I.T., Cambridge, Mass., 1977) and *Men's Studies Bibliography* (M.I.T., Cambridge, Mass., 1977).

MCGREGOR, O.M., The Social Position of Women in England 1850–1914: A Bibliography (*The British Journal of Sociology* **6** 1955).

MCGUIGAN, D.G., *New Research on Women* (University of Michigan, Centre for the Continuing Education of Women, Ann Arbor, 1974).

NIEVA, V.F. and GUTEK, B.A., *Women and Work: A Bibliography of Psychological Research* (Catalogue of Selected Documents in Psychology, May 1976, Vol. 6).

OLSON, D. *Bibliography of Sources Relating to Women* (The Department of State, Lansing, Michigan, USA, 1975).

RADER, H. and BUTTERFIELD, M., *The Role of Women in Society* (The University Library, East Michigan, 1971).

ROBY, P. and PATTERSON, M., *Women in Society: A Bibliography* (The Department of Sociology, Brandeis University, Waltham, Massachusetts, 1972).

ROSENBERG, M.B. and BERGSTROM, L.V., *Women and Society: A Critical Review of the Literature with a Selected Annotated Bibliography* (Sage, London, 1975).

ROWBOTHAM, S., *Women's Liberation and Revolution: A Bibliography* (The Falling Wall Press, Bristol, 1973).

RUTGERS UNIVERSITY, EAGLETON INSTITUTE OF POLITICS, CENTRE FOR THE AMERICAN WOMAN AND POLITICS, *Women and American Politics: A Selected Bibliography 1965–1974* (Rutgers University Press, New Brunswick, New Jersey, 1974).

RUZEK, S.K., *Women and Health Care* (The Program on Women, Northwestern University, Evanston, Illinois, June 1975).

SHIELDS, P., BREINICH, S. and KOHEN, A., *Women and the Economy: A Bibliography and a Review of the Literature on Sex Differentations in the Labour Market* (The College of Administrative Science, Centre for Human Resource Research, Ohio State University, 1975).

SOLTOW, M.J., *American Women and the Labour Movement 1825–1974: An Annotated Bibliography* (The Scarecrow Press, Metuchen, New Jersey, 1976).

US GOVERNMENT PUBLICATIONS: *US Working Women: A Databook* (US Dept. of Labour, Bureau of Labour Statistics, 1977); *Sexism and Racism*, and *Women and Poverty* (US Commission on Civil Rights, 1974); *Women in Management: Selected Recent References* (US Dept. of

Labour, 1978), *Resources in Women's Educational Equity* (US Dept. of Health, Education and Welfare, 1977). The latter is a comprehensive and annotated bibliography of issues relevant to women: employment, education, health, etc. It is available from the Women's Educational Equity Communications Network, 1855 Folson Street, San Francisco, California 94108, USA).

VELIMESIS, M.L., The Female Offender (*Crime and Delinquency Literature* **7** 1974).

VERGAEGEN, R.C., *La Condition de la Femme dans la Vie Quotidienne* (Les Ours, Brussels, 1971).

WHEELER, H., *Womanhood Media: Current Resources about Women* (The Scarecrow Press, Metuchen, New Jersey, 1972).

WHITE, W. (ed.), *The North American Reference Encyclopaedia of Women's Liberation* (North American Publishing Company, Philadelphia, Pennsylvania).

WOMEN AND LITERATURE, *An Annotated Bibliography of Women Writers* (available from the Sense and Sensibility Collective, 57 Ellery Street, Cambridge, Mass. 02138).

WOMEN AND LITERATURE, *A Bibliography* (published by the Department of English, Douglass College, New Brunswick, New Jersey, 08903).

GENERAL REVIEWS OF LITERATURE

BALLOU, P., Bibliographies for Research on Women (*Signs* **3** (2): 436-450, Winter 1977).

BERKOWITZ, T., MANGI, J.M., WILLIAMSON, J., (eds.) *Who's Who and Where in Women's Studies* (The Feminist Press, Old Westbury, New York, 1974).

BOULDING, E., NUSS, S., CARLSON, D.L., GREENSTEIN, M., (eds.) *Handbook of International Data on Women* (Sage, London, 1977).

EHRICH, C., The Woman Book Industry (*American Journal of Sociology* **78** (4) January, 1973).

GUELAND-LERIDON, FRANCOISE, *Recherches sur la Condition Feminine dans la Société d'Aujourd'hui* (Presses Universitaires de France, Paris, 1967).

HOCHSCHILD, A.R., A Review of Sex Role Research *American Journal of Sociology* **78** (4): 1011-1029, January 1973).

LERNER, Gerda (ed.) *Black Women in White America: A Documentary History* (Vintage, New York, 1973).

LERNER, Gerda, (ed.) *The Female Experience: An American Documentary* (Bobbs-Merrill, Indianapolis, 1977).

MEAD, M. and KAPLAN, F.B. (eds.), *American Women: Report of the President's Commission on the Status of Women and Other Publications of the Commission* (Charles Scribner, New York, 1965).

STAFFORD, Beth, Researching Women's Studies: A Guide (*Women's Studies* **1**: 117-26, 1978).

WOLFF, JANET, Women's Studies and Sociology (*Sociology* **11**: 155–61, January 1977).

FEMINIST JOURNALS AND PERIODICALS

AMAZON QUARTERLY (Box, 434, West Somerville, Mass. 02144, USA).

CANADIAN NEWSLETTER OF RESEARCH ON WOMEN (Department of Sociology, Ontario Institute for Studies in Education, 252, Bloor Street West, Toronto, Canada, M5S IV6).

FEMINIST ART JOURNAL (941, Montgomery Place, Brooklyn, N.Y., 11215, USA).

FEMINIST REVIEW (65 Manor Road, London, N.16).

FEMINIST STUDIES (417, Riverside Drive, New York, N.Y., 10025, USA).

FRONTIERS (Journal of the Women's Studies Programme, University of Colorado, and available from Hillside Court, Apt. 104, Boulder, Colorado, 80309, USA).

HECATE (c/o, The English Department, University of

Queensland, St. Lucia, Brisbane 4067, Queensland, Australia).

M/F (69, Randolph Avenue, London W9 IDW).

MS (370, Lexington Avenue, New York, N.Y., 10017, USA).

NOW (Monthly Newsletter of the National Organisation of Women, 46 East 91st Street, New York, N.Y., 10028, USA).

OFF OUR BACKS (1724, 20th Street N.W., Washington, D.C. 20009, USA).

PAPERS IN WOMEN'S STUDIES (The Women's Studies Program, Ann Arbor, Michigan, 48109, USA).

PSYCHOLOGY OF WOMEN: A QUARTERLY (The Editor, Department of Psychology, California State University, Hayward, California 94542, USA).

QUEST: A FEMINIST QUARTERLY (Box 8843, Washington, D.C., 20003, USA).

QUESTIONS FEMINISTES (1, Rue des Fosses Saint Jacques, Paris 75005, France).

SIGNS (The University of Chicago Press, 11030 Langley Avenue, Chicago, Illinois, 60628, USA).

SPARE RIB (27, Clerkenwell Close, London EC1).

SPOKESWOMAN (5464, South Shore Drive, Chicago, Illinois, 60615, USA).

WOMEN (3028, Greenmount Avenue, Baltimore, USA).

WOMEN AND HEALTH (Biological Sciences Program, State University of New York College at Old Westbury, Box 210, Old Westbury, N.Y., 11568).

WOMEN'S REPORT (14, Aberdeen Road, Wealdstone, Middx.).

WOMEN'S RESEARCH AND RESOURCES CENTRE: NEWS-LETTER (Available from the WRRC, 190, Upper Street, London, N.1).

WOMEN'S RIGHTS LAW REPORTER (Transaction Periodicals Consortium, Rutgers University, New Brunswick, New Jersey, 08903).

WOMEN'S STUDIES (The Pergamon Press, Oxford, England).

# Author index

Acker, J., 11
Adamson, O., 10
Adler, F., 40, 41
Aken, C., 26, 27
Alexander, S., 21, 22
Allen, J., 52
Allen, S., 10, 11, 16, 18, 22, 26, 30
Allendorf, M., 56
American Psychological
    Association, 64
Amir, M., 43
Angel, J., 25
Anderson, K., 37
Anthropological Quarterly, 53
Appadorair, A., 53
Archer, J., 55, 59
Archibald, K., 25
Ardener, E., 50, 51
Astin, H., 25
Atkinson, T., 4
Auerbach, N., 46

Bachofen, J., 47
Bacon, M., 60
Baker, E., 49
Baker, L., 31
Baker Miller, J., 65
Bailyn, L., 60
Banks, J., 7
Banks, O., 7
Banner, L., 30
Bardwick, J., 58, 59, 61

Barker, D., 10, 11, 16, 18, 22, 26,
    30
Barker-Benfield, B., 62
Barnett, H., 42
Barnett, J., 24
Barrett, C., 65
Barron, R., 22
Barry, H., 60
Bart, P., 11, 30, 65
Basch, F., 46
Bass, B., 22
Baum, M., 18
Baym, N., 46
Baxandall, R., 37
Bean, J., 59
Bebel, A., 3
Beck, E., 25
Becker, G., 22
Beechey, V., 22
Bell, C., 18
Bell, W., 65
Benet, J., 25
Benet, M., 46
Benston, M., 3, 10, 15
Berg, B., 7
Berg, P., 65
Bernard, J., 18, 24, 25
Bernikow, L., 46
Berquist, V., 37
Bieri, J., 59
Bird, C., 4
Blackstone, T., 25, 31

Blaxall, M., 22
Blom-Cooper, L., 36
Boals, K., 37
Borges, S., 43
Boston Women's Health Book
    Collective, 28, 29
Boring, P., 31
Boserup, E., 53
Bott, E., 18
Bourque, S., 37
Boxer, M., 56
Bradburn, W., 59
Breen, D., 62
Bridenthal, R., 11
Brierley, J., 31
Briller, S., 4
Brisson, R., 40
Brittain, V., 31
Brody, W., 14
Broverman, I., 60, 65
Brown, B., 15
Brown, C., 10
Brown, G., 64
Brown, J., 51
Brown, P., 53
Brown, R., 22
Brownlee, M., 22
Brownlee, W., 22
Brownmiller, S., 43
Bruegel, I., 23
Bryan, J., 42
Buchbinder, G., 53
Bujra, J., 53
Bullough, V., 42, 47
Burgers, A., 43
Burman, S., 36
Burniston, S., 62
Byrne, E., 31

Calder, J., 46
Calderwood, A., 27
Callahan, S., 24
Caplan, P., 53
Carden, M., 3, 8
Carlson, R., 59
Carroll, B., 11
Centre for Women's Policy Studies,
    43

Chafe, W., 7
Chapman, J., 22, 35
Chesler, P., 65
Chetwynd, J., 34
Chesney-Lind, M., 35
Child, I., 60
Chiplin, B., 23
Christoffel, T., 10
Clark, A., 21
Clark, C., 15
Clark, S., 27
Clarkson, F., 61
Coleman, R., 17
Cohler, C., 65
Comer, L., 18
Cook, A., 37
Cook, F., 29
Coonz, C., 11
Cooper, L., 10
Coote, A., 35
Corea, G., 29
Coser, R., 23
Cott, N., 21
Coulson, M., 16
Courtney, A., 45
Coussins, J., 35
Coward, R., 59, 65
Cowie, E., 40, 65
Cowie, J., 40
Critique of Anthropology, 51
Croll, E., 56
Crow, D., 21
Cunningham, M., 55
Cuvillier, R., 16

Dahlstrom, E., 53
Dalla Costa, M., 5, 15, 16
Daniels, A., 36, 37, 46
Davidoff, L., 17, 18
Davies, Margery, 21
Davies, Margaret, 25
Davies, M., 10
Davin, D., 56
Davis, K., 42
De Beauvoir, S., 4
Decrow, K., 36
Deem, R., 31
Deere, C., 53

Degler, C., 63
Delaney, J., 29
Delphy, C., 10, 18
Dennis, N., 13
Department of Education and Science, 31
Deutsch, H., 59
Dewey, L., 37
De Winter, M., 26
Dixon, M., 3, 8
Dodge, N., 56
Donnison, J., 25
Douglas, M., 51
Douvan, E., 61
Draper, P., 53
Dreitzel, P., 18, 19
Duchan, L., 26
Dumoulin, J., 16

Eaton, E., 65
Edwards, R., 10
Ehrenreich, B., 29
Ehrhardt, A., 60
Elbert, S., 48
Eifler, D., 62
Eisenstein, Z., 10
Eliade, M., 48
Ellis, J., 59
Elliott, P., 26
Ellman, M., 46
Elston, M., 25
Engels, F., 10, 51
English, D., 29
Epstein, C., 25, 37
Eriksson-Joslyn, K., 37
Evans, R., 7
Evans-Pritchard, E., 50
Ewbank, I., 46

Farber, S., 61
Farrer, C., 48
Faulk, M., 43
Fava, S., 25
Fee, E., 50, 51
Fee, T., 16
Feagin, J., 33
Figes, E., 2, 5
Firestone, S., 2, 5

Flora, C., 45
Fogarty, M., 18
Fox, D., 62
Frankenberg, R., 11
Frankfort, E., 29
Frazer, R., 17
Frazier, N., 31
Fredeman, W., 21
Freeman, J., 3, 9
Freud, S., 59
Friedan, B., 2, 5
Friedl, E., 51
Friedman, L., 45
Friedman, R., 59
Froschl, M., 61
Fryer, P., 29
Fulton, O., 25
Furniss, W., 26

Gail, S., 17
Galinsky, D., 59
Gallant, D., 65
Galway, K., 27
Garai, J., 59
Gardiner, J., 16, 33
Garfinkel, A., 36
Gaskof, M., 5, 9
Gates, M., 35
Gauger, W., 15
Gavron, H., 17
Gayford, J., 43
Gelles, R., 43
Gerstein, I., 15, 16
Gevhardt, P., 63
Giele, J., 51, 53
Gill, T., 35
Gillespie, D., 18
Gilman, C., 2, 3
Githens, M., 37
Glassman, C., 33
Glastonbury, M., 48
Glazer-Malbin, N., 5, 15
Glover, E., 42
Goldberg, M., 10, 23
Goldmann, E., 3
Goode, J., 46
Goode, W., 19, 44
Goody, J., 36

Goot, M., 37
Gordon, L., 29
Gornick, V., 5, 64
Goulianos, J., 46
Gove, W., 64
Grabiner, E., 10
Graham, P., 31
Graham, S., 26
Gray, J., 29
Greenstein, F., 37
Greenwald, H., 42
Greenwood, V., 29
Greer, G., 2, 5
Griffin, S., 26, 43
Grimm, J., 23
Gross, E., 23
Grossholtz, J., 37
Grunebaum, H., 64
Guettel, C., 5
Guilbert, M., 23
Gutman, D., 61

Hacker, H., 10
Hall, R., 7
Hamilton, R., 10
Handel, G., 17
Hanmer, J., 30, 33, 53
Hardwick, E., 47
Hartnett, O., 34
Harris, T., 64
Harrison, G., 41
Harrison, J., 16
Hartman, M., 30, 65
Haskell, M., 45
Hays, H., 48
Hedges, J., 24
Heidensohn, F., 40
Heilbrun, C., 5
Henley, N., 48
Henriques, F., 13, 42
Herschberger, R., 5
Hess, T., 49
Hewitt, M., 21
Hibey, R., 36
Hill, C., 1, 7
Himmelweit, H., 16
Hirsch, W., 7
Hite, S., 63

H.M.Government, 33, 44
Hobsbawm, E., 20
Hobson, D., 17
Hoffman, L., 24, 61
Hoffman, M., 63
Hoffman-Bustamente, D., 41
Holcombe, L., 21
Hole, J., 9
Hollingsworth, L., 63
Holme, A., 24
Holstrom, L., 43
Hope, E., 26
Hordern, A., 29
Horner, M., 60, 61
Horney, K., 59, 63
Horobin, G., 29
Hunt, J., 9
Hutt, C., 58 59

Iglitzin, L., 33

Jacklin, C., 60
Jackson, S., 43, 63
Jacobs, S., 51
James, S., 5, 15, 16
Jefferys, M., 26
Johnson, V., 63
Johnston, J., 2, 6
Johnstone, C., 45

Kaberry, P., 53
Kamm, J., 7, 32
Kanowitz, L., 26, 36
Kanter, R., 11, 26, 41
Kaplan, A., 59
Kaplan, S., 47
Kauffer, K., 10
Kennedy, M., 26
Kennie, A., 4
King, J., 45
Kinsey, A., 63
Kirkpatrick, J., 37
Klein, D., 41
Klein, V., 24, 61
Knudsen, D., 9
Komarovsky, M., 19, 60, 61
Koedt, A., 4, 6, 63
Konopka, G., 40

Koppelman, S., 49
Kreps, J., 23
Kress, J., 41
Krusell, J., 22
Kuhn, A., 10

La Fontaine, J., 51
Lakoff, R., 48
Land, H., 33, 34
Landes, J., 16
Lamphere, L., 52
Laslett, P., 14
Laurenson, D., 47
Leavith, R., 54
Leeson, J., 29
Lefcourt, C., 36
Legman, C., 48
Leith-Ross, S., 54
Lenin, V., 4
Lennane, A., 30, 65
Lennane, R., 30, 65
Lerguia, I., 16
Lerner, G., 14
L'Esperance, J., 18
Levi, J., 62
Levine, E., 6, 9, 54
Levine, R., 54
Levy, B., 32, 61
Lewin, A., 26
Liddington, J., 7
Lifton, R., 47
Linton, R., 54
Lipman-Bluman, J., 48
Lipshitz, S., 65
Lister, R., 34
Llewellyn, C., 26
Lloyd, B., 55, 59
Lloyd, C., 23
Lobodzinska, B., 56
Lockeretz, S., 45
Lombroso, C., 39, 40
Lopata, H., 17
Lopate, C., 26
Lupton, M., 29
Luy, M., 30

Maccoby, E., 59, 60
Macintyre, S., 63

Mackie, L., 23
Mackintosh, M., 16
Madden, J., 23
Magas, B., 9, 16, 37
Maher, V., 54
Man, J., 65
Mandel, W., 56
Manton, J., 7
Marceau, J., 19
Marder, H., 47
Marks, E., 47
Marks, P., 32
Marsh, D., 19
Martin, C., 63
Masters, W., 63
Mathieu, N., 11
Mattfeld, J., 26, 27
Matthiasson, C., 54
Mayo, M., 33, 34
McCall, R., 54
McCourt, K., 37
McRobbie, A., 61
Mead, M., 52
Medea, A., 43
Mellen, J., 46
Merkle, J., 56
Mernissi, F., 54
Merton, R., 42
Middleton, C., 10
Milburn, J., 38
Milden, J., 14
Mill, J.S., 1, 3
Millett, K., 2, 6, 42, 47
Millman, M., 11, 41
Millum, T., 46
Mintz, S., 54
Mitchell, J., 2, 11, 18, 21, 31, 37, 60
Mitchell, M., 26
Moberley-Hill, E., 7
Moers, E., 8, 49
Mohun, S., 16
Money, J., 60
Moore, J., 38
Moran, B., 5, 64
Morewedge, R., 54
Morgan, R., 6, 33
Mort, F., 62
Moulton, R., 65

Murdock, G., 52
Murphy, Y., 54
Myrdal, A., 24

Navarro, V., 30
Neff, W., 21
Nelson, A., 38
Newby, H., 18
Newcomer, M., 32
Newton, N., 63
Nightingale, C., 47
Nilsen, A., 47
Nisbet, R., 42
Nochlin, L., 49
Norris, G., 22
Norris, J., 7
N.S.P.C.C., 44
Nye, F., 24

Oakley, A., 17, 18, 21, 30, 31, 37
Oates, M., 32
O'Donovan, K., 36
Oleson, V., 62
Olsen, T., 49
O'Neill, W., 7
Oppenheimer, V., 23
Ortner, S., 52

Pahl, J., 44
Pankhurst, S., 7
Parkin, F., 11
Parsons, J., 62
Parsons, T., 19
Pattullo, P., 23
Peel, J., 30
Perl, J., 41
Perucci, C., 26
Petersen, K., 49
Phillips, A., 29
Pinchbeck, I., 20, 21
Pizzey, E., 44
Polk, B., 9
Pollak, O., 40
Pomeroy, L., 65
Pomeroy, S., 54
Pomeroy, W., 63
Porter, M., 54
Potts, M., 30

Prestage, J., 37
Price, J., 10
Pruitt, I., 56
Pugh, M., 7

Quataert, J., 56

Radcliffe, M., 3
Rainwater, L., 13, 17
Rakusen, J., 29
Raphael, E., 38
Rapone, A., 6
Rapoport, R., 18, 62
Rapoport, R.N., 18, 62
Rattray, R., 52
Reagan, B., 22
Reed, E., 11
Reich, M., 10
Reid, E., 37
Reiter, R., 52
Rendel, M., 35, 36
Reynolds, J., 43
Rich, A., 64
Richards, E., 21
Roberts, H., 47
Roby, P., 32
Rogers, S., 52, 54
Robins, E., 63
Rosaldo, M., 50, 52
Rose, C., 8
Rose, H., 30
Rosen, A., 8
Rosenberg, C., 14
Rosenblatt, P., 55
Rosenblum, K., 41
Rosenkranz, P., 61
Rossi, A., 6, 9, 26, 27
Roszak, B., 6
Roszak, T., 6
Rowbotham, S., 2, 6, 38, 56
Rowntree, J., 11
Rowntree, M., 11
Rubington, E., 42
Ruether, R., 45
Ruina, E., 27
Rukoff, G., 23
Russell, D., 43
Rutgers University, 38
Ruzek, S., 29, 37

Sachs, A., 36
Sadker, M., 31
Safilios-Rothschild, C., 9, 12, 52
Saghir, M., 63
Salaff, J., 56
Sanger, M., 4
Schaeffer, D., 59, 60
Scharf, B., 11
Scheinfield, A., 59
Schiller, A., 27
Schlegel, A., 52
Schneir, M., 4
Schreiner, O., 2, 4
Schuck, V., 38
Schulder, D., 36
Scott, A.F., 8
Scott, A.M., 8
Scott, C., 30
Scott, H., 56
Scott, J., 18
Scully, D., 30
Secombe, W., 15, 16
Shanley, M., 38
Shainess, N., 62
Shaw, J., 32
Sharpe, S., 32
Shepher, J., 55
Sherman, J., 60
Shorter, E., 14, 21
Showalter, E., 47
Shulman, A., 4
Signs, 32, 55
Simms, M., 30
Simon, R., 27, 39
Slater, E., 40
Slaughter, C., 13
Sloane, P., 23
Slocum, S., 50, 52
Smart, B., 36, 41
Smart, C., 36, 41
Smelser, N., 20
Smith, A., 36
Smith, D., 17, 30
Smith, R., 27
Smock, A., 53
Smuts, R., 21
Snow, H., 56
Solanas, V., 6

Spacks, P., 47
Spring-Rice, M., 18
Social Problems, 24
Solomon, B., 62
Steinman, A., 62
Stern, R., 23
Stites, R., 8
Stoller, R., 60
Stone, L., 14
Stopes, M., 4
Stott, M., 45
Strachey, R., 8
Strathern, M., 55
Straus, M., 44
Stuard, S., 55
Sullerot, E., 55
Sutherland, S., 62
Suval, E., 40
Szymanski, A., 3, 11, 17

Tavistock Institute, 27
Tavard, G., 48
Taylor, L., 8
Theodore, A., 27, 61
Thirsk, J., 36
Thomas, K., 8
Thomas, W., 40
Thompson, D., 38
Thompson, E., 20, 36
Thompson, K., 43
Thompson, R., 55
Thonnerson, W., 8
Thorne, B., 48
Tiger, L., 55
Tilly, L., 18
Tomalin, C., 8
Toner, B., 43
Toomey, D., 18
Toren, N., 34
Toth, E., 29
Tresemer, D., 62
Trilling, L., 47
Trotsky, L., 4, 19
Tuchman, G., 46, 49
Tudor, J., 64

UNESCO, 32

Van Aken, J., 26, 27
Van Allen, J., 52
Vanek, J., 15
Vaz, E., 40
Vedder, C., 40
Venning, C., 34
Vicinus, M., 21
Vincent, C., 64
Vogel, T., 15, 17, 61
Volgy, T., 38

Waehrer, H., 5
Wainwright, H., 16
Waite, L., 24
Wakefield, P., 3
Wall, R., 14
Walton, R., 34
Wandor, M., 6, 64
Ward, B., 55
Warner, M., 48
Watson, B., 47
Weedon, C., 62
Weinbaum, B., 56
Weinberg, M., 42
Weir, A., 44
Weis, K., 43
Weiss, B., 65
Weisstein, N., 64
Weitzman, L., 62
Wertheimer, B., 21, 38

White, C., 46
White, M.S., 27
Whiting, P., 64
Williams, J., 27
Williamson, S., 32
Willis, E., 17
Willmott, P., 19
Wilson, E., 33, 34
Wilson, J., 49
Wilson, R., 61
Winn, D., 42
Winship, J., 46
Wipper, A., 55
Wise, N., 40
Wolf, M., 57
Wollstonecraft, M., 1, 3
Wolpe, A., 10, 32
Women's Studies Group, 17, 46, 61, 63
Woolf, V., 48, 49

Young, J., 29
Young, M., 19, 57
Youssef, N., 55
Yudkin, S., 24

Zaidi, S., 55
Zaretsky, E., 19
Zola, I., 30
Zollschen, G., 7